D0086562

"Authentic Assessment

Designing Performance-Based Tasks"

Katherine "Luongo-Orlando"

Thomas J. Bata Library
TRENT UNIVERSITY WITHDRAWN
PETERBOROUGH, ONTARIO

LIBRARY
CURRICULUM
COLLEGE
TRENT UNIVERSITY
WITHDRAWN

Pembroke Publishers Limited

Curric LB 1576 .L 857 2003

To my sisters, for sharing life and our educational journey.

To my youngest angel: May the world inspire you to be a lifelong learner.

© 2003 Pembroke Publishers
538 Hood Road
Markham, Ontario, Canada L3R 3K9
www.pembrokepublishers.com

Distributed in the U.S. by Stenhouse Publishers
477 Congress Street
Portland, ME 04101
www.stenhouse.com

All rights reserved.
No part of this publication may be reproduced in any form or by any means
electronic or mechanical, including photocopy, recording, or any information,
storage or retrieval system, without permission in writing from the publisher.

We acknowledge the financial support of the Government of Canada through the
Book Publishing Industry Development Program (BPIDP) for our publishing
activities.

We acknowledge the Government of Ontario through the Ontario Media
Development Corporation's Ontario Book Initiative.

National Library of Canada Cataloguing in Publication

Luongo-Orlando, Katherine
    Authentic assessment: designing performance-based tasks for achieving language
arts outcomes / Katherine Luongo-Orlando.

Includes bibliographical references and index.
ISBN 1-55138-152-4

    1. Language arts (Elementary). 2. English language — Study and teaching
(Elementary). I. Title.

LB1576.L857 2003   372.6'044   C2002-906053-2

Editor: Kate Revington
Cover Design: John Zehethofer
Cover Photography: Ajay Photographics
Typesetting: Jay Tee Graphics Ltd.

Printed and bound in Canada
9 8 7 6 5 4 3 2 1

Contents

Planning Authentic Performance Tasks

Imagine a classroom where children actively engage in rich, complex, and diverse experiences that interest and inspire them. Picture them embarking upon real-world challenges, resolving complex problems, and taking part in authentic learning situations. Envision these young people using problem-solving, reasoning, critical thinking, and learning skills in practical and astonishing ways. The creative tasks that children accomplish in these rich environments enable them to produce writing, projects, experiments, presentations, exhibitions, portfolios, and other innovative products of their learning.

As students engage in such programs, teachers need to develop a comprehensive and precise method of assessing the knowledge, skills, and work habits that students demonstrate. Students themselves should play a leading role in creating assessment and evaluation procedures that shape their learning and measure the quality of their work.

Authentic Assessment is an effort to help teachers in elementary classrooms implement performance-based learning and authentic assessment practices throughout the curriculum. It emerged out of my own classroom experiences with students. The assessment units and performance tasks featured here transpired from years of teaching and learning with young people of diverse backgrounds and different ability levels. The practical strategies and examples are meant to provide models for program development and assessment design. Whether you are new to performance-based learning and authentic assessment, or interested in enhancing learning and current practices, this resource should provide you with practical, creative, and inspiring ideas to use in your teaching.

The Nature of Authentic Assessment

Since planning authentic assessment begins with understanding the language, conceptual frameworks, and developments in the assessment and evaluation field, in the section below, you will find comprehensive definitions, explanations, and thoughtful clarification on related topics referred to throughout this book.

What is the difference between assessment and evaluation?

Assessment is the process of gathering information about student learning. A variety of methods (e.g., observation, discussion, checklists, and anecdotal reports) are used to collect data about student performance. The task of gathering information is shared by teachers and students. The data collected through the application of systematic and purposeful techniques forms the basis of evaluation of student achievement.

Evaluation is the process of judging information gathered through assessment and of making decisions about the quality of student performance. By reviewing the evidence collected through assessment, teachers can determine the value of final products and assign a score or grade for reporting purposes.

What is the purpose for assessment and evaluation?

Assessment and evaluation practices are designed to meet distinctive educational goals and objectives. During this period of educational change, diagnosis, program evaluation, accountability, and student placement are some of the factors driving assessment and evaluation. (Specific objectives will be addressed throughout this book.)

What types of assessment and evaluation are there?

- *Diagnostic assessment and evaluation* occurs at the beginning of the school year, term, unit, or period of time when students are experiencing difficulty. By gathering data and making judgments, teachers can determine students' prior knowledge, capabilities, attitudes, learning styles, motivational levels, interests, strengths, and instructional needs in order to design effective programs.

- *Formative assessment and evaluation* plays an integral part of the learning process as students engage in instructional activities and assessment tasks throughout the school year. Techniques, notably observations, checklists, conferences, and discussions, are used to offer feedback to students about work in progress or developing skills. Information gathered through formative assessment and evaluation is used to determine student progress, improve performance, and modify instruction.

- *Summative assessment and evaluation* takes place at the end of a unit of study, course, term, or period of time when students are prepared to demonstrate their understanding and application of curriculum objectives. Data collected by such methods as self- and peer-assessments are used to make judgments about the value of student work.

Developing a balanced and comprehensive evaluation program requires consistent and frequent use of all three types of assessment and evaluation. Using a variety of measures, including diagnostic, formative, and summative techniques, places a much-needed emphasis on both the processes and products of learning. Allowing students to demonstrate their understanding and skills in several ways, as well as employing a range of assessment strategies, helps improve performance and create a detailed portrait of each child as a learner throughout the year.

What is authentic assessment?

In this period of accountability, alternative methods of assessment are being introduced in classrooms to determine the quality of students' work. *Authentic assessments* involve students in tasks that require the application of knowledge and skills in real-life situations. These alternative methods offer real-world challenges and frameworks, such as audiences, for demonstrating concepts and strategies that students have learned. Authentic assessments, rooted in classroom instruction, address educational goals and groups of learning objectives. These practices place a greater emphasis on problem solving, critical thinking, comprehension, reasoning and metacognition, or self-reflection, skills than traditional assessment techniques. Final products include portfolios, exhibitions, performances, investigations, experiments, journals, presentations, and other open-ended formats that permit more than one solution. The formats for student work recognize students' multiple intelligences, different learning styles, and varying developmental levels.

What is performance-based learning and assessment?

Performance-based learning and assessment is an authentic method of instruction and evaluation whereby students apply knowledge and skills through practical demonstrations or creative products that illustrate learning. Performance tasks present learners with real-world challenges that require them to synthesize and apply the concepts, strategies, and work habits they have developed through classroom instruction to authentic assessment situations. During a unit of study, students are provided with exemplary learning experiences designed to build the knowledge base and skill level needed for the assessment. Throughout the performance task, learners are expected to perform an activity, produce a response, or create a product that demonstrates their competencies in a variety of complex ways. For example, they might prepare written works, oral discourses, exhibitions, experiments, or projects. Performance assessments offer a creative format for evaluating student understanding.

What is the rationale for developing performance-based assessments?

For years, traditional methods of assessment and standardized testing have been used in schools to measure student progress. The limitations of such techniques as pencil-and-paper tests or multiple choice examinations have increased the demand for alternative assessments. Most traditional tests rely heavily on factual knowledge and conceptual understanding; however, these methods do not accurately measure students' problem-solving, reasoning, and critical thinking skills or recognize work habits, ability to cooperate, or sense of responsibility. The limitation of standardized tests and other traditional assessment techniques has also made it difficult to determine the capabilities of students not coping in the mainstream. In many cases, conventional methods of evaluation have distracted these, and other, children from the learning process. Furthermore, the scope of traditional testing may be presented in a context that seems isolating and irrelevant to some students, making it hard for them to apply the content they have learned.

In order to help students become motivated, independent learners who know and use essential concepts, learning skills, and work habits, teachers are implementing authentic assessment practices in their classrooms. These alternative assessments encompass a wide range of activities and presentation formats that provide in-depth information about students' progress. Performance tasks enable students to demonstrate a richer level of understanding and application of process and learning skills in a broader context than traditional testing would allow. Authentic assessments provide a practical framework for displaying concepts and strategies learned. The close links to instruction help create a context for evaluation that is related to the educational goals of the curriculum.

What is the place of performance-based learning and authentic assessment in the curriculum?

Performance-based learning and alternative assessment practices are an integral part of a balanced curriculum and a comprehensive assessment program. Studies in education by such leading researchers as Davies, Cameron, Politano, and Gregory (1992), along with Wiggins and McTighe (1998), indicate that authentic assessment must be an essential component in the overall evaluation of student progress. Because authentic assessment is rooted in the curriculum, teachers can focus instruction on learning experiences designed to prepare students for the performance task. Literature, current events, and thematic units of study can effectively be used to organize the curriculum and plan performance tasks.

How are performance assessments scored?

Student performance from authentic assessment is often measured by standards and objectives related to the curriculum. The results are judged against specific criteria that learners know prior to the assessment. Students' progress is determined over time as samples are collected in a portfolio or other work collection for evaluation and reporting purposes. Unlike many traditional assessment methods, performance assessments are scored by people, not machines. To provide an accurate measure of achievement, a variety of holistic and analytic scoring methods — observations, checklists, rating scales, and more — are used to assess final products.

A Guide to Planning Performance-Based Assessments

Designing as well as conducting authentic assessments presents a new challenge for educators. Developing effective assessments may require a shift from traditional methods towards approaches that focus on the learning process, the final product, or actual student performance. Many teachers may find that learning activities they are already doing can be shaped into authentic performance tasks. Beginning with these classroom projects may make the development process easier for those new to performance-based assessment. To be most effective, this assessment method should be used for complex projects or culminating activities for a unit of study. Strategically placing these performance tasks at the end of a series of lessons or a unit will allow students to build on earlier content knowledge, process skills, and work habits.

A systematic guide to planning performance-based classroom assessments follows. Subsequent chapters expand upon this outline.

Step 1: Set focus goals and identify learning outcomes, purpose, and audience.

Planning authentic assessments begins with the establishment of a focus goal that will guide both instruction and evaluation. To establish a focus goal, review learning expectations from curriculum documents and program guidelines. Identify common outcomes, including key concepts and essential skills, to be assessed. Group related educational objectives together, perhaps by highlighting expectations. Identify the enduring understandings, for example, appreciation of literature, in each set of expectations, and use these to determine an overall goal. Inform students of the focus goal so they are aware of the main objective of the unit, performance task, and assessment. Be sure to explain it clearly.

Next, revisit the curriculum documents and program guidelines for the grade level, subject, or unit being taught. Identify the knowledge, skills, and work habits (e.g., time management, cooperation, and sense of responsibility) that are to be assessed. Specify learning objectives from each discipline area related to the focus goal. Develop a list of curriculum expectations that students are to acquire, practise, and demonstrate during the unit and performance task. The list of related content, skills, and attitudes can be generated individually, or with a team of teachers assigned to the same grade, discipline area, or division. Prior to the assessment, share the learning outcomes with school administrators, staff members, parents, students, and other interested audiences as much as is expected at your particular school.

Later, determine a purpose for the assessment. The primary goal of assessment and evaluation is to improve student learning. Performance-based assessment, and other methods of evaluation, may be specifically conducted

- to determine students' prior knowledge, skills, and work habits, perhaps for diagnostic purposes
- to identify individual strengths and weaknesses
- to track student progress over time
- to provide information about student progress and achievement to students, parents, schools, and other stakeholders
- to determine final grades, student placement, and student eligibility for a program certificate
- to develop students' skills in self-assessment and reflection, and
- to plan, implement, and improve instructional practices, curriculum, and educational programs

Finally, select an audience for the performance task. Establishing an audience for student work will motivate learners to perform their best and prepare them for real-life tasks that have an audience. To promote independence, allow students to select their own audiences when appropriate. Possible audiences may include teachers; peers; students in other classrooms or schools; parents/guardians and other family members; the principal, librarian, or other school staff; and volunteers, guest speakers, and advocacy groups.

Consider completing an outline such as that beginning on page 12 which provides an example of a specific focus goal and set of learning objectives. A blank copy of the full form, titled Performance-Based Assessment Planning, appears as an appendix.

Step 2: Develop a performance task that will assess the learning outcomes.

The assessment task should be aligned with the focus goal and match the learning objectives and curriculum expectations. Select or design a performance-based activity that requires students to demonstrate their understanding of content, knowledge of concepts, application of process skills, and related work habits or attitudes. Contextualize the task in order to provide learners with an authentic situation that exemplifies real life.

Literature, current events, and themes from social studies and other subject areas can be used as a context to develop a performance-based activity. Selecting an authentic audience and realistic format for student work can extend a performance activity into a real-world task that engages young people and motivates them to learn.

To design an effective performance task for your students, be sure to consider the nature, interests, and overall work habits of the class, as well as the needs of individual students.

Consider, too, whether you want to take a discipline-based or integrated approach to curriculum development and assessment design. Constructing multidimensional tasks that combine learning experiences from different subject areas enables teachers to assess several disciplines at once.

Finally, consider offering a range of presentation formats as options for how students can demonstrate their learning. A list of formats appears on page 11. Planning for a variety of formats and allowing young people to choose their own presentation tools help support students' varying learning styles and multiple intelligences and enable all children to succeed in developmentally appropriate ways.

Once you have developed an assessment task, review it to ensure that it meets these criteria:

- There is a focus on learning expectations and curriculum outcomes.
- The task assesses a variety of knowlege and skills (e.g., cognitive, reasoning, problem-solving, comprehension, critical thinking, metacognitive, affective, and social).
- It is fair and free of bias, inclusive, and adaptable for diverse students, including those with special needs.
- The task allows students to perform at various levels of achievement and present their learning using different formats.
- It is based on teachable, observable, and measurable learning experiences.
- It is practical and credible.
- Implementation, in terms of time, space, equipment, and costs, is feasible.
- The task is multidimensional or interdisciplinary.

Completing Performance-Based Assessment Planning sheets, where you note the focus goal, learning objectives, task description, and classroom preparation required for effective implementation and results, should help you. A sample is featured on pages 12–14, and a photocopiable version appears as an appendix.

Presentation Formats

Newspaper
Magazine
Multimedia presentations:
• slide show
• Web site
• digital pictures
Commercial
Radio broadcast
TV segment
Documentary
TV/Radio news program
Media tools:
• editorial
• comics/cartoons
• advertisement

Primary documents:
• first-hand accounts
• letters
• diary
• journal
• historical news clippings

Biography
Trivia game
Timeline
Reports (e.g., news, lab)
Research project
Essays
Photo essay
Instructions/Guidebook
Brochures
Picture books
Myth
Legend
Fairy tale
Folktale

Visual displays
• murals
• paintings
• posters
• drawings
• diagrams
• illustrations
• sketches
• print making
• bulletin board
• exhibits
Oral presentation using visual aids (e.g., overheads)
Investigations
Demonstrations
Experiments

Puppets
Play
Dramatization
Pantomime
Choral speaking
Improvisation
Role play
Writing in role
Dance sequence
Ensemble
Musical composition
Poem
Song/Rap
Masks
Scroll
Artifacts
Sculpture
Carving
Maps
Short musical
Soundtrack
Storyboard

Computer generated charts and graphic organizers:
• list
• flowchart
• charts
• graphs
• spreadsheets
• database
• table
• census
• histogram
• stem and leaf plots
• Venn diagram

Panel discussions
Group discussions
Talk show
Debate
Film/video
Film strip
Slides (photos)
Photographs
Audio recording
Interview
Survey

Towers
Bridges
Structures
Models
3D figures
Information cube
Puzzle

© 2003 *Authentic Assessment* by Katherine Luongo-Orlando. Pembroke Publishers. All rights reserved. Permission to reproduce for classroom use.

Performance-Based Assessment Planning

Focus Goal: *To use non-fiction sources to conduct research on a topic and various presentation methods/tools to report information*

Learning Objectives/Outcome/Expectations
(content/knowledge, skills, work habits or attitudes)

- *develop research skills*
- *read and understand a variety of non-fiction materials*
- *formulate questions to gain information*
- *gather information using different inquiry methods*
- *locate relevant information from a variety of sources*
- *communicate research findings using different presentation tools and methods*

Task Description

Purpose:

to track student progress over time

Audience:

teacher, librarian, parents, peers

Performance Activity:

Students will select a research topic related to a unit of study, conduct non-fiction research and report information using various presentation methods or tools of their choice.

Instructional Activities

Introduce students to various types of non-fiction.

Teach lessons on important research skills, such as
- selecting a topic
- formulating questions
- developing a focus
- gathering information
- reading non-fiction
- understanding new vocabulary and concepts
- recording information (e.g., note taking skills)
- noting references
- organizing content

Introduce/review various methods and presentation tools that can be used to report research findings, such as oral and written reports, multimedia presentations, and informational posters/diagrams.

Model the use of research strategies and provide opportunities for students to practise research skills with others.

Have students practise presenting research information in a variety of ways.

Assessment/Evaluation Tool
(scoring procedure)

Research Skills Rubric

Directions to Students
(Example: prompts, questions)

Select a research topic related to a unit you are currently studying in class. Use the steps in the research process to locate information on your topic from different non-fiction sources. Present your research findings using a method or presentation tool of your choice.

Presentation Options/Response Modes

Research findings and information can be presented
  in oral or written reports
  in different genre formats (e.g., magazine, newspaper)
  using multimedia tools and equipment (e.g., slide show)
  in a visual display (e.g., poster, museum exhibit)

Other Important Considerations (Identify and list.)

Materials and Equipment:

a variety of non-fiction sources including primary documents, print materials (reference/resource books, information technology (CD-ROMs)
audio/visual/electronic and computer equipment (e.g., digital camera)

Resources:

Harvey, S. Nonfiction Matters: Reading, Writing and Research in Grades 3-8. Portland, Maine: Stenhouse Publishers, 1998.
Luongo-Orlando, K. A Project Approach to Language Learning: Linking Literary Genres and Themes in Elementary Classrooms. Markham, Ontario: Pembroke Publishers, 2001.
Portalupi, J., and R. Fletcher. Nonfiction Craft Lessons: Teaching Information Writing K-8. Portland, Maine: Stenhouse Publishers, 2001.

Time Allotment: _2-3 weeks_

Classroom Organization

Individual Tasks:

Select a research topic related to a unit of study, conduct non-fiction research using the process and strategies introduced, and present information using a method of their choice.

Work in Partners/Pairs:

Locate a variety of sources of non-fiction to be included in a classroom resource centre and display.
Practise questioning, interview, and recording strategies.

Small-Group Activities:

Practise research skills and present information on various topics using a variety of methods and presentation tools (oral reports, multimedia, etc.).

Large-Group/Whole-Class Activities:

Introduce research process and important skills and strategies for using non-fiction to conduct research.
Model the research process and strategies.
Introduce, demonstrate, and use various presentation tools.

Step 3: Develop and implement a unit of study that will prepare students for the performance task.

The instructional activities should provide background information and introduce essential content, skills, and work habits required during the assessment. The unit of study and classroom lessons ought to reflect the focus goals and curriculum expectations. They form the foundation for the assessment.

To prepare students for the assessment, gather resources, plan classroom activities, and teach lessons related to the learning objectives. To check that they have the prerequisite knowledge, skills, and attitudes needed for the performance task, use a range of assessment tools — conferences, portfolios, observations, anecdotal notes, checklists, and more — to track individual progress. See Chapter 3 for a selection of instructional activities grouped under three units of study.

Step 4: Design scoring procedures and assessment tools that will be used to measure students' achievement on the performance task.

Identify the scoring criteria that will be used to determine the level of performance on the assessment task. Select the standards for judging students' achievement by providing models of student work. Examine the samples and discuss the characteristics of each level of performance. Outline the expectations for the assessment prior to implementation. Develop a scoring process, rating scale, or method for assessing final products. Assessment tools that can be used to measure students' achievement on the performance task include these:

- *analytic scale,* where score points are assigned to specific criteria
- *attitudinal scales,* where students rate their attitudes, preferences, and opinions about a subject, skill, or topic such as reading
- *anecdotal notes,* where comments and observations of students are recorded by the teacher in point form or as jot notes
- *holistic scale,* where a generic score is assigned to a student's final product using a common set of guidelines or descriptors
- *point system,* where score values are assigned to performance characteristics
- *developmental continuum,* where a student's performance level is determined by a set of stages, or phases, of development
- *checklist,* which offers a list of performance features, or behaviors, to be observed and checked off
- *observations,* where a teacher pays attention to how students work, apply skills, and interact with others by engaging in tasks with them, noting behaviors, and listening to children at work
- *progress tracking sheet/chart,* which keeps a record of the growth or steps in completing a performance task
- *interview,* where a questioning strategy is used to elicit information about student performance
- *conference,* where a discussion is held with an individual or group of students about their learning and overall performance
- *portfolio,* where a collection of work samples are compiled and stored over time
- *self, peer, or group assessments,* where students reflect on their performance and assess their own work and that of others, using established criteria without assigning themselves a grade
- *performance contract,* which is an agreement made by the student to meet the requirements of a performance task

- *performance task assessment list*, where the quality of a performance is judged according to a detailed list of criteria, and analytic scores are assigned to each
- *rubric*, a scoring tool used to assess and evaluate the quality of student performance based on a scaled set of grading criteria featuring narrative descriptions or performance guidelines
- *progress report*, a formal evaluation record of a student's overall achievement over a period of time where letter grades or marks may be assigned
- *scoring sheets*, where analytic or holistic methods are used to judge the quality of student performance

See Chapter 2 for information on designing rubrics.

Step 5: Introduce the performance task and administer the assessment.

Prior to implementation, inform students of the focus goal, establish the learning expectations, review the scoring criteria, and specify the assessment procedures. Provide learners with directions to guide them through the performance task. Then administer the assessment. Instructions for featured tasks can be found in Chapter 4.

Step 6: Gather evidence and score results.

Throughout the assessment process, gather evidence of students' achievement by making observations, holding conferences, and reviewing drafts and revisions. Once students have finished their performance tasks, have them conduct self- and peer-assessments. Use the scoring procedures developed previously to assess (or evaluate) the final products, determine grades, and summarize the results. Provide feedback to students, parents, and other audiences, as required. Chapter 5 elaborates on this step.

Step 7: Promote reflection and goal setting in students.

Have students reflect on their performance, note progress, determine strengths and weaknesses, and set goals for improvement. Tools for reflection may include anecdotal response sheets, checklists, learning or response logs, goal setting journals, questionnaires, inventories, portfolio entries, reflective letters, and reflective classroom discussions. A variety of tools are presented in Chapter 6.

Step 8: Interpret and use the results.

Gather samples of students' work that will help you to determine standards of performance for future assessments. Examine students' levels of achievement and overall performance. Interpret the results and draw inferences from the assessment. Use this evidence to determine program implications and plan modifications to the curriculum, instructional practices, allocation of resources, testing and assessment methods and procedures. Revisit the purposes outlined for the performance task in order to ensure that the results have been used appropriately. Reflect on the observations noted throughout the design and implementation process. You will find the experiences acquired in administering each performance task essential in planning effective assessments in the future. Chapter 7 addresses the issue of interpreting and communicating results.

The chapter concludes with a chart summary of the process of planning assessment and designing a performance task.

Steps in Planning Assessment and Designing a Performance Task

STEP 1: Initial Planning
- Set focus goals and identify learning outcomes, purpose, and audience.
  Review Chapter 1.

STEP 2: Performance Task Design
- Develop a performance task that will assess the learning outcomes.
- Consider the interests of the class and the individual needs of students.
- Select or design a format for the final product.
- Identify the learning materials, equipment, resources, time allotment, and other program considerations.
  Review Chapter 1.

STEP 3: Assessment Tool Design
- Design scoring procedures and assessment tools that will be used to measure students' achievement on the performance task.
- Develop assessment tools and select scoring criteria with students, colleagues, or independently.
- Locate exemplars or determine standards for excellence.
- Share assessment strategies, scoring criteria, and tools with students prior to implementation.
  See Chapter 2.

STEP 4: Curriculum Development
- Review the performance task requirements carefully and identify the essential concepts, skills, and work habits that need to be taught.
- Develop units of study and plan lessons that will prepare students for the assessment.
- Provide students with learning experiences and instructional activities that will impart the prior knowledge, skills, and work habits required for the performance task.
- Make program modifications where necessary to accommodate students' needs.
- Use a variety of assessment tools to track students' progress throughout the unit.
  See Chapter 3.

STEP 5: Administration
- Introduce the performance task and administer the assessment.
- Share the focus goal, learning outcomes, assessment tools, and scoring criteria with students beforehand.
- Provide directions that will guide students throughout the assessment.
- Schedule sufficient time and locate adequate resources and learning materials.
  See Chapter 4.

STEP 6: Data Collection
- Gather evidence of student learning using a range of techniques.
  See Chapter 5.

STEP 7: Reflection
- Have students engage in self-assessment, reflection, and goal setting using various tools.
  See Chapter 6.

STEP 8: Evaluation and Reporting
- Evaluate students' achievement on the performance task using the assessment tools that have been developed.
- Consider students' self-assessments and reflections when determining final scores.
- Share results with others by providing essential feedback to students, parents, and other audiences using a variety of conference formats or communication methods.
- Interpret and use the results for different purposes, such as making program modifications.
- Use the observations, information, and experiences acquired in administering the performance task to plan future assessments.
  See Chapter 7.

2

Developing Assessment and Evaluation Tools

Performance-based learning requires the construction of assessment tools and evaluation instruments designed to measure quality and indicate overall levels of achievement. In recent years, rubrics have become one of the most common scoring methods used to rate student performance. A *rubric* places students' work on a continuum of quality based on narrative descriptions or criteria guidelines that indicate different levels of performance. When shared with students, such an instrument becomes a powerful tool to motivate students to work towards a high level of performance.

When designing a rubric for evaluating an authentic performance task, strive to do the following:

• Match evaluative criteria with the focus goal and curriculum expectations.
• Express the criteria in clear and simple language that students can understand.
• Present levels of performance in affirmative ways.
• Include specific, measurable characteristics of performance.
• Summarize evaluative criteria and levels of performance within a page or two.
• Use a scoring scale with three to five levels to rate student performance.

Creating an assessment rubric can be a challenging task for educators. Working with a colleague or group of teachers can make the development process easier. Students should also be involved in the construction of rubrics that will be used to assess their performance.

Begin with one curriculum area at a time and introduce rubrics gradually. Use rubrics to assess student performance on major projects, activities, presentations, and performance tasks. By following the steps provided below, you can create an assessment rubric for classroom use.

How to Create a Rubric

Step 1: Review the focus goal and curriculum expectations identified previously.

Consider the major learning outcomes and performance task requirements. Note the important concepts, specific skills, and key behaviors that should be demonstrated throughout the assessment.

Step 2: Determine the evaluative criteria that will be used for judging student performance on the task.

These will be general or task specific. The evaluative criteria selected should reflect the instructional goals of the assessment task and represent teachable and observable performance characteristics. To select criteria, examine samples of students' work with the class and discuss the features of quality work. Produce a list of scoring criteria based on models of excellent performance. If student samples are unavailable, consider the attributes of exemplary performance or quality production in order to determine the evaluative criteria to be used.

Note the general or task-specific criteria that will later appear on the rubric template. A general scoring rubric will include a generic list of features or performance characteristics that should be used to judge the students' response. For example, for a writing task it may include such generic criteria as content, organization, sentence construction, mechanics, and language usage. A task-specific rubric will identify the precise requirements for a specific performance task. For a visual arts task on creating a sculpture, it may include such precise criteria as preparation, form/representation, use of medium, craftsmanship, originality, aesthetic value, and critique.

Step 3: Establish the performance standards for different achievement levels.

Share examples of students' work at a variety of levels with the class. Discuss the features of work at different levels of performance. List the traits for each achievement level based on the evaluative criteria. If student samples are unavailable, determine the characteristics of different performance levels based on knowledge of common errors/problems, possible omissions, or other factors that may affect work quality.

Step 4: Write a description of each level of performance with the class.

Invite learners to make suggestions for performance descriptors in order to ensure the gradations of quality are written in language that students understand. Be sure to vary the descriptors to signify the different performance levels. The performance indicators should include the specific attributes or features that define each achievement level. These levels should also parallel one another and reflect a different degree of mastery of the same skills (e.g., "makes few/occasional/frequent spelling errors"). Where possible, the standards of performance for each level should be accompanied by models or examples.

Step 5: Develop a scoring procedure to be used in rating student performance on the assessment task.

A scoring strategy may be either analytic or holistic.

An *analytic strategy* examines several traits or criteria in the student's response. These rubrics include separate ratings for each element. To develop and use an analytic scale, score points are assigned and given to different aspects of the student's work. The criterion-by-criterion scores may or may not be accumulated into an overall score. Although the results are quantitative, these rubrics should not evaluate the quantity of items. In other words, it would be inappropriate to note number of spelling errors, reading miscues, number of resources, and so on in the final product or actual student performance. To ensure fairness and reliability, teachers should use quantitative rubrics periodically to offer feedback when conducting diagnostic and formative assessment, for example.

A *holistic strategy*, on the other hand, takes all of the evaluative criteria into consideration or examines only one trait in the student's response. Here, a single score, grade, or rating is given to the student's work. To develop and use a holistic scoring method, a generic score is assigned to the final product based on the overall quality of performance. The evaluator makes a general judgment of the work using a common set of guidelines or descriptors. These qualitative results are often used for summative evaluation purposes.

Depending on the type of strategy selected, a rubric format will need to be developed. Some effective formats are as follows:

- a numerical scale, which offers an analytic rating, such as 1 to 4
- a qualitative scale, where descriptive categories define each level
- a point system, where score points are assigned to performance features
- letter grades, where, for example, achievement levels are indicated by A, B, C, D
- a performance checklist, or a list of elements of quality performance
- a developmental continuum based on stages/phases of development

After establishing the rubric format that will be used to rate the quality of students' work, select the terms that define each achievement level. Remember to describe the levels of performance in affirmative ways, such as the following:

- developing, beginning, needs assistance to
- capable, developing, beginning
- level four, level three, level two, level one
- A, B, C, D
- exemplary, proficient, progressing, or not meeting the standard
- excellent, good, satisfactory, needs improvement
- full accomplishment, substantial accomplishment, partial accomplishment, little or no accomplishment
- emergent, beginning, developing, independent, fluent levels
- exemplary achievement, commendable achievement, adequate achievement, limited achievement, minimal achievement, no response

Step 6: Construct the rubric by designing a template, or frame, that can be adapted for different assignments.

Fill in the performance criteria (general or task specific). Match the scoring method selected (e.g., numerical or descriptive scale) and the rubric terms to the descriptions of each level of performance.

Step 7: Use the rubric for self- and peer-assessment and teacher evaluation.

Provide students with copies of the rubric developed together and ask them to assess their own progress on project work and performance tasks. Encourage learners to use the rubric to rate the student samples or models introduced previously. Challenge them to use the criteria from the rubric to examine the work of peers. The rubric can be used effectively to promote learning by providing students with standards to improve their performance. However, assigning score points, rating scales, letter grades, or other symbols should remain your responsibility alone.

Step 8: Review, revise, edit, and publish the final rubric.

Ensure through discussion that students understood the rubric language and were able to use it effectively to determine the quality, level, or standard of performance. Clarify any terms and make modifications where necessary. Reach classroom consensus on rubric terms and scoring procedures. Make revisions and edit the rubric where required. Publish the final rubric. Share a copy with students, parents, administrators, and other interested audiences. Use the final rubric to determine students' results on the performance-based assessment task.

Introduction to Three Assessment Units

Performance Tasks Listed by Assessment Unit

Making Connections with Literature
- Writing a Sequel
- Oral Retelling

Exploring a Universal Concept: Community
- Making a Community or Historical Map
- Developing a Want Ad
- Scheduling Life in the Community
- Making Community Goods and Providing Directions

Understanding the Influence of Advertising
- Developing a Product
- Creating Body Copy
- Designing an Ad Layout
- Packaging a Product

The assessment units featured in this book have been organized around literature, community, and the media.

The performance tasks, assessment and evaluation tools, and instructional activities included are interdependent. The performance tasks that have been developed for each of the assessment units are featured in Chapter 4, Administering the Assessment. Task requirements and assessment procedures are described on the pages Instructions for Students in the same chapter. Learning activities designed to prepare students for the performance tasks provide the focus of Chapter 3, Planning Instructional Activities. The assessment and evaluation tools for each of the performance tasks are located in this chapter, Chapter 2. Remember to establish the assessment and evaluation strategy *before* implementing the assessment.

Take, for example, the featured theme Understanding the Influence of Advertising. To plan an assessment unit around it, select a related performance task from the list at left or the more detailed overview chart on page 40. Once you have chosen a performance task, such as Developing a Product (page 91), locate the corresponding assessment and evaluation tool in this chapter, perhaps Performance Checklist for Packaging a Product (page 33). Review and share the performance criteria and assessment and evaluation strategy with your students. Then, locate the instructional activities featured in Chapter 3; these will prepare learners for the performance task. Provide students with the knowledge, skills, and work habits required for the performance task by teaching the appropriate lessons and providing time for the instructional activities. Finally, administer the assessment following the guidelines in Chapter 4, Administering the Assessment.

Several assessment and evaluation tools pertaining to the ten performance tasks featured in this book appear on pages 22 to 36. The scoring procedures and rubric formats that have been designed can be used exclusively or adapted for other performance tasks. For teachers interested in developing their own assessment and evaluation tool for a performance task, the process of designing a rubric, which is described in detail in this chapter, is summarized on page 37 for easy reference.

Performance Assessment List for Writing a Sequel

Student's Name: _____ Date: _____

Title of Chosen Narrative: _____

		Assessment Points	
		Possible Points	Earned Points
The story sequel meets these criteria:			
_____	Basic elements of story from the original text (setting, character, plot, and theme)	4	_____
_____	Detailed descriptions of the setting	3	_____
_____	Accurate character portrayals	6	_____
_____	Plot developments that unfold logically from the original narrative	6	_____
_____	Related story conflicts and resolutions	4	_____
_____	Dialogue throughout the story	5	_____
_____	Reasonable predictions	3	_____
_____	Effective style of writing, literary devices, and language that flows well with the existing story	5	_____
_____	Logical organization of ideas and continuation of events, in other words, no unexplained "gaps"	6	_____
_____	Additional details and creative ideas that extend the original story (e.g., new characters, settings)	3	_____
_____	Correct and consistent use of language conventions (e.g., spelling, grammar, and punctuation)	5	_____
	TOTAL	50	_____

© 2003 *Authentic Assessment* by Katherine Luongo-Orlando. Pembroke Publishers. All rights reserved. Permission to reproduce for classroom use.

Performance Assessment List for Writing a Sequel
Scoring Guidelines

To use the assessment list and score the performance accurately, carefully review the student's work or sample and identify the assessment criteria included.

   Quality of performance and final score points can be determined by locating evidence of each criterion, or element, in the final product. Assign points to each element based on evidence using the guidelines below.

- Assign one point for each story element (setting, character, plot and theme) identified correctly in the sequel (maximum 4 points).

- The story sequel should contain vivid details that enable the reader to visualize or produce a realistic illustration of the setting. Assign one score point for each detail included to describe the setting (maximum 3 points).

- The story sequel should accurately describe at least two main characters featured in the original story. Each character description should include at least two related details that help portray the character vividly. Details might focus on physical appearance, background, age, role, interests, or habits. Assign one score point for each main character identified and additional points for the character details included in the sequel (maximum 6 points).

- The plot of the sequel should be richly developed. Events should unfold logically based on the original text. A well-developed sequel should contain basic plot elements, such as opening event, rising action, climax, falling action, resolution, and culminating event. Assign one score point for each component of plot development included in the sequel (maximum 6 points).

- The story sequel should be based on realistic conflicts that characters encountered in the original story or related problems they may face in similar situations. Solutions to story conflicts should be described in the sequel too. Assign score points for each problem, solution, or piece of related information, such as reasons or a cause-and-effect relationship, included in the sequel (maximum 4 points).

- Writing a sequel to an existing story requires students to make reasonable predictions. The story sequel should be a logical continuation of events. Assign score points for the facts and evidence used from the original narrative to make predictions and produce the sequel (maximum 3 points).

- The story sequel should feature dialogue between characters. Including dialogue in a narrative requires the ability to use language conventions, including quotation marks, capitalization, and other forms of punctuation, correctly. Narrative conversations should also use active words and appropriate vocabulary, have an authentic sense of voice, include relevant content, and reflect patterns of human speech. Assign score points for each feature of story dialogue included in the sequel (maximum 5 points).

© 2003 *Authentic Assessment* by Katherine Luongo-Orlando. Pembroke Publishers. All rights reserved. Permission to reproduce for classroom use.

Scoring Guidelines (cont.'d)

- A well-written sequel should flow logically and stylistically with an existing story. Students can adopt an author's writing style by using literary devices and language from the original text in their own narratives. Examine the use of imagery; literary devices, such as similes and metaphors; diction, which includes connecting words and words that create mood; and other elements of distinctive writing found in the sequel. Assign score points for each (maximum 5 points).

- The story sequel should have a logical organization of ideas. A well-developed narrative should have a clear introduction, middle, and conclusion and feature important episodes or main events. Assign 1 score point for an effective beginning, 3 score points for related episodes, and 1 score point for an effective ending to the sequel (maximum 5 points).

- A story sequel should include engaging details, interesting information, and creative ideas that extend the story. Assign score points for relevant information, additional facts, important details, and explanations not included in the original text that will assist readers in better understanding the story (maximum 3 points).

- A story sequel should feature the consistent and accurate use of language conventions and compositional elements. Examine the student sample, and find evidence of the overall application of grammar and punctuation rules, spelling patterns, paragraphing, sentence variety and accepted sentence structure. Deduct a score point for each major error in language usage and mechanics. (For example, a student sample with several major errors in spelling should lose one score point for spelling, *not* one point for each spelling error.) (maximum 5 points)

© 2003 *Authentic Assessment* by Katherine Luongo-Orlando. Pembroke Publishers. All rights reserved. Permission to reproduce for classroom use.

Performance Assessment List for Oral Retelling

Student's Name: _____   Date: _____

Title of Chosen Narrative: _____

Type of Retelling (circle one):   Guided   Unguided

	Assessment Points	
	Possible Points	Earned Points
Story Structure		
Includes an effective introduction, middle, and conclusion	3	_____
Elements of Story		
Refers to basic narrative elements (setting, characters, plot, and theme)	4	_____
Setting		
Provides information about time and place Includes vivid details about the setting (at least 2)	4	_____
Characters		
Identifies the main character of the story Includes supporting details about the main character Mentions other characters in the narrative and explains their role and/or characteristics	6	_____
Problem		
Refers to main character's conflict or goal	1	_____
Plot		
Explains main events/episodes (at least 3) Presents story events/episodes in a logical sequence	6	_____
Resolution		
Explains the resolution to the problem or achievement of the main character's goal	1	_____
Theme		
States theme, main topic, or message of the story	1	_____
Language and Diction		
Reflects style of the original narrative Uses similar vocabulary and literary devices	4	_____
TOTAL	30	_____

© 2003 *Authentic Assessment* by Katherine Luongo-Orlando. Pembroke Publishers. All rights reserved. Permission to reproduce for classroom use.

Self-Assessment Rubric for Story Sequel or Oral Retelling

Title of Story Sequel or Oral Retelling: _____

Note: This rubric is intended to promote critical reflection, not to be used for a recorded grade.

Grade   Criteria

A   I read the original story independently.

           I began my story sequel or oral retelling with an effective introduction.

           I used a complex and logical structure to develop my sequel or retelling.

           I included a well-developed middle and ending.

           I included descriptive and vivid details about the setting.

           I identified the characters accurately and described them in detail.

           I identified the different story problems/conflicts correctly and explained related solutions.

           I included many important story episodes, plot developments, and events.

           I described events in sequential order and avoided unexplained gaps consistently.

           I made reasonable predictions.

           I included dialogue in my sequel or retelling.

           I understood the theme, main topic, or message of the story clearly.

           I included many added details and creative ideas in my sequel that flow well with the original story. (I introduced many new characters, story problems, and interesting events.)

           I used clear, precise, and expressive vocabulary consistently.

B   I read the original story independently.

           I began my story sequel or oral retelling with an appropriate introduction.

           I used a logical structure to develop my sequel or retelling.

           I included a fairly well-developed middle and an ending.

           I included accurate descriptions of the setting.

           I identified the characters accurately and described them in some detail.

           I identified most story problems/conflicts correctly and explained related solutions.

           I included most important story episodes, plot developments, and events.

           I described events in sequential order and avoided unexplained gaps most of the time.

           I made appropriate predictions.

           I included some dialogue.

           I understood the theme, main topic, or message of the story somewhat clearly.

           I included several added details and creative ideas in my sequel that flow well with the original story. (I introduced several new characters, story problems, and interesting events.)

           I used clear, precise, and expressive vocabulary most of the time.

© 2003 *Authentic Assessment* by Katherine Luongo-Orlando. Pembroke Publishers. All rights reserved. Permission to reproduce for classroom use.

Self-Assessment Rubric (cont.'d)

Grade Criteria

C   I read the original story with limited assistance.

I began my story sequel or oral retelling with a simple introduction.

I used a basic structure to develop my sequel or retelling.

I included a simple middle and an ending.

I included some accurate descriptions of the setting.

I identified some characters accurately and described them with few details.

I identified some story problems/conflicts correctly and occasionally explained related solutions.

I included some story episodes, plot developments, and events.

I described events in some logical order and avoided some unexplained gaps.

I made some accurate and reasonable predictions.

I included little dialogue in my sequel or retelling.

I understood the theme, main topic, or message of the story in a limited way.

I included some added details and creative ideas in my sequel that flow well with the original story. (I introduced some new characters, story problems, and interesting events).

I used simple vocabulary.

D   I read the original story with assistance.

I began my story sequel or oral retelling with a limited introduction.

I developed my sequel or retelling incompletely.

My story lacks a logical middle and/or ending.

I included few descriptions of the setting.

I identified few characters accurately and described them with little, if any, detail.

I identified a few story problems/conflicts correctly and rarely explained related solutions.

I included few story episodes, plot developments, and events.

I did not describe events in a logical or sequential order.

My sequel or retelling contained many unexplained gaps.

I made few accurate predictions.

I included no dialogue.

I had difficulty understanding the theme, main topic, or message of the story.

I included few, if any, added details and creative ideas in my sequel that flow well with the original story. (I introduced few, if any, new characters, story problems, and interesting events.)

I used limited vocabulary.

© 2003 *Authentic Assessment* by Katherine Luongo-Orlando. Pembroke Publishers. All rights reserved. Permission to reproduce for classroom use.

Community Map Evaluation Sheet

Student's Name: _____ Date: _____

Rating Scale:

	5 Excellent	4 Good	3 Satisfactory	2 Limited	1 Needs Improvement

Criteria		**Rating**			
Title Specifies the topic and appears neatly at the top of the map	5	4	3	2	1
Content Features accurate information, including landmarks and places, related to the topic	5	4	3	2	1
Appearance Uses color/shading on areas of the map neatly and appropriately	5	4	3	2	1
Legend/Labels Includes appropriate symbols or labels that are well positioned and accurate	5	4	3	2	1
Other Features Indicates cardinal directions and uses scale to represent distance or location on a map	5	4	3	2	1

Comments:

© 2003 *Authentic Assessment* by Katherine Luongo-Orlando. Pembroke Publishers. All rights reserved. Permission to reproduce for classroom use.

Writing Evaluation Sheet

Student's Name: _____ Date: _____

Type of Writing (circle one): Classified Ad Procedure Schedule Other

Rating Scale:	5	4	3	2	1
	Excellent	Good	Satisfactory	Limited	Needs Improvement

Criteria **Rating**

Criteria	5	4	3	2	1
Writing Process Follows the steps in the writing process (prewriting activities, rough drafts, editing/revision, final copy)	5	4	3	2	1
Content Includes accurate information, complete explanations, and adequate details related to the topic	5	4	3	2	1
Organization/Development Develops logically in an ordered sequence	5	4	3	2	1
Visual Presentation and Format Presents content in a structured layout/format that is easy to read	5	4	3	2	1
Language Usage Uses appropriate vocabulary and effective word choices suited to the purpose and type of writing (e.g., technical, subject-specific)	5	4	3	2	1
Application of Language Conventions Applies knowledge of spelling, grammar, and punctuation rules consistently and accurately	5	4	3	2	1

Comments:

© 2003 *Authentic Assessment* by Katherine Luongo-Orlando. Pembroke Publishers. All rights reserved. Permission to reproduce for classroom use.

Writing Rubric

Criteria	Levels of Achievement			
	Level 1	Level 2	Level 3	Level 4
Preparing and Planning	uses few, if any, strategies to plan texts and prepare for writing tasks (discusses ideas with others)	uses some strategies to plan texts and prepare for writing tasks (brainstorms ideas, uses jot notes)	uses a number of strategies to plan texts and prepare for writing tasks (brainstorms ideas, uses jot notes, discusses ideas with others)	uses a wide variety of strategies to plan texts and prepare for writing tasks (conducts research, brainstorms ideas, develops outlines, discusses ideas with others)
Purpose	writes for limited purposes (to entertain)	writes for some different purposes (to entertain, instruct)	writes for a number of different purposes (to entertain, instruct, persuade, explain)	writes for a wide variety of purposes (to entertain, instruct, persuade, explain, inform, reflect)
Form and Genre Convention	uses a limited number of writing formats (narratives, reports) and genre conventions (descriptive)	uses some different writing formats (narratives, reports, instructions) and genre conventions (descriptive, informative)	uses a number of writing formats (narratives, reports, instructions, explanations) and genre conventions (descriptive, informative, explanatory)	uses a wide variety of writing formats or genre conventions (narratives, reports, instructions, explanations, expositions) and genre conventions (descriptive, informative, explanatory, persuasive)
Audience Awareness	writes for limited audiences (self, teacher)	writes for some different audiences (self, teacher, parents)	writes for a number of audiences (self, teacher, parents, peers)	writes for a wide variety of audiences (self, teacher, parents, peers, school staff, school community)

© 2003 *Authentic Assessment* by Katherine Luongo-Orlando. Pembroke Publishers. All rights reserved. Permission to reproduce for classroom use.

Writing Rubric (cont.'d)

Criteria	Levels of Achievement			
	Level 1	**Level 2**	**Level 3**	**Level 4**
Organizational Development	few ideas flow logically; content is developed and explained in a limited way	some ideas flow logically; content is minimally developed and explained	most ideas flow logically; content is fairly well developed and explained	all ideas flow logically; content is fully developed and explained
Sentence Structure	writes limited or simple sentences with several errors and very little variety	uses some correct sentence structure with little variety	uses correct sentence structure with some degree of variety	uses correct and varied sentence structure consistently
Vocabulary	uses limited vocabulary that lacks clarity, precision, or expression	uses appropriate vocabulary; sometimes includes clear or expressive word choices	uses clear, precise, vivid and expressive vocabulary most of the time	uses clear, precise, vivid and expressive vocabulary consistently
Spelling, Grammar, Punctuation	contains several errors in spelling, grammar, and punctuation	contains some errors in spelling, grammar, and punctuation	contains few errors in spelling, grammar, and punctuation	contains very few, if any, errors in spelling, grammar, and punctuation

Comments:

© 2003 *Authentic Assessment* by Katherine Luongo-Orlando. Pembroke Publishers. All rights reserved. Permission to reproduce for classroom use.

Performance Checklist for Creating Body Copy

Student's Name: _____ Date: _____

E Excellent   **G** Good   **S** Satisfactory   **N** Needs improvement

Performance Criteria	Results			
The student:	E	G	S	N
Uses the writing process effectively to produce the body copy that will appear on the printed advertisement (writing rough drafts, editing, revising, conferencing, and publishing)				
Includes a headline, slogan, and testimonials as part of the body copy (text on the print ad)				
Writes a complete product description (summary, purposes/uses, important details, distinguishing features) of the consumer good developed				
Uses a variety of effective words, phrases, and expressions from the ad word bank and other vocabulary resources				
Presents ideas and information logically in sequence where required (e.g., for product descriptions, or instructions)				
Use persuasive writing to convince others				
Reduces language to compact, effective phrasing				
Selects words appropriate to the target audience and type of appeal (factual, emotional, or sensory)				
Provides additional information in the body copy (contest descriptions, entry forms, promotional offers, contact information)				

Comments:

© 2003 *Authentic Assessment* by Katherine Luongo-Orlando. Pembroke Publishers. All rights reserved. Permission to reproduce for classroom use.

Performance Checklist for Packaging a Product

Student's Name: _____   Date: _____

E Excellent   **G** Good   **S** Satisfactory   **N** Needs improvement

Performance Criteria	Results			
The student:	E	G	S	N
Features labels (product name), visuals (photo, illustration), and graphics (logos) on package design				
Applies visual elements and symbols to graphic designs on packages (lettering, size of print, color, lines, shapes)				
Constructs own product package using appropriate materials and design methods/procedures				
Includes complete set of procedures or instructions describing how to use the product as part of package design				
Describes procedures or instructions in a logical sequence				
Provides additional information on product package (quantity, promotional offers, nutritional information)				

Comments:

© 2003 *Authentic Assessment* by Katherine Luongo-Orlando. Pembroke Publishers. All rights reserved. Permission to reproduce for classroom use.

Performance Checklist for Designing an Ad Layout

Student's Name: _____ Date: _____

E Excellent	**G** Good	**S** Satisfactory	**N** Needs improvement

Performance Criteria	Results			
The student:	E	G	S	N
Includes common layout features (headline, slogan, product description, visuals, graphic logo, brand name label) on the print advertisement				
Selects or designs appropriate visuals (photo or illustration) for the layout featuring the product package or product in use				
Applies visual elements and symbols to graphic design features on ad layouts (lettering, size of print, color, shapes on logos)				
Selects an appropriate page format, arrangement, and size for the ad				
Uses an effective appeal on the ad layout to attract potential buyers (factual, emotional, or sensory)				
Features additional items on the ad layout (testimonial, product character, contact information)				

Comments:

© 2003 *Authentic Assessment* by Katherine Luongo-Orlando. Pembroke Publishers. All rights reserved. Permission to reproduce for classroom use.

Performance Checklist for Developing a Product

Student's Name: _____   Date: _____

E Excellent   **G** Good   **S** Satisfactory   **N** Needs improvement

Performance Criteria	Results			
The student:	E	G	S	N
Demonstrates an understanding of the product development process (involving consumers, conducting market research, selecting a target audience, choosing an appeal)				
Plans and conducts market research, surveys, product testing, and sampling				
Develops a consumer product, brainstorms a list of names, identifies product purpose, outlines its uses, and highlights important features				
Selects an appropriate sales technique (famous person, product character, familiar experience) to promote the product				
Chooses a suitable target audience for the consumer product created				
Uses an effective appeal to attract members of the target audience (factual, emotional, or sensory)				
Other:				

Comments:

© 2003 *Authentic Assessment* by Katherine Luongo-Orlando. Pembroke Publishers. All rights reserved. Permission to reproduce for classroom use.

Oral Presentation Rubric

Criteria	Levels of Achievement			
	Level 1	Level 2	Level 3	Level 4
Communication of Knowledge/ Concepts	shares limited or irrelevant information, provides incomplete or no explanations, demonstrates limited understanding of concepts	shares general or partially relevant information, provides partially complete explanations, demonstrates general understanding of concepts	shares relevant information, provides complete explanations, demonstrates solid understanding of concepts	shares comprehensive and interesting information, provides complete and accurate explanations, demonstrates thorough understanding of concepts
Clarity of Voice	expresses little content clearly and precisely	expresses some content clearly and precisely	expresses most content clearly and precisely	expresses all content clearly and precisely
Vocabulary and Language Usage (e.g., conventions, grammar)	rarely uses appropriate vocabulary and proper language conventions	occasionally uses appropriate vocabulary and proper language conventions	usually uses appropriate vocabulary and proper language conventions	consistently uses appropriate vocabulary and proper language conventions
Audience Awareness	rarely maintains eye contact with listeners/audience	occasionally maintains eye contact with listeners/audience	usually maintains eye contact with listeners/audience	consistently maintains eye contact with listeners/audience
Attitude/ Disposition	seems to lack confidence, appears nervous, remains unfocused, does not have proper posture	displays some confidence, appears somewhat calm and focused, is beginning to maintain proper posture	displays confidence most of the time, appears quite calm and focused, maintains proper posture most of the time	demonstrates confidence, appears calm, remains focused, maintains proper posture consistently
Organization	rarely presents content/ideas in a logical sequence	occasionally presents content/ideas in a logical sequence	usually presents content/ideas in a logical sequence	always presents content/ideas in a logical sequence
Visual Aids (e.g., charts, tables, props, overheads)	uses few, if any, presentation methods and media tools effectively	uses some presentation methods and media tools effectively	uses several presentation methods and media tools effectively	uses a variety of presentation methods and media tools effectively

© 2003 *Authentic Assessment* by Katherine Luongo-Orlando. Pembroke Publishers. All rights reserved. Permission to reproduce for classroom use.

Designing a Rubric Summary

- Review the focus goal and curriculum expectations addressed by the performance task.

- Select the scoring criteria (general or task specific) that will be used for judging student performance.

- Establish the performance standards for different achievement levels.

- Write a description of each performance level noting the performance indicators (characteristics of each level).

- Develop a scoring procedure (analytic or holistic) to be used in rating student performance on the assessment task.

- Devise a rubric format (e.g., scale, point system, letter grades, checklist).

- Select the terms that define the levels of performance.

- Design a template, or frame, for the rubric.

- List the performance criteria and fill in the performance indicators.

- Record the scoring method and rubric terms that describe each level of performance on the rubric template.

- Use the rubric for self- and peer-assessment and teacher evaluation.

- Revise, edit, and publish the final rubric that will be used to determine the results of the performance task.

Planning Instructional Activities

Performance-based learning challenges young people to develop curriculum expectations and apply background knowledge, skills, and work habits in authentic assessment situations.

First of all, children should have an opportunity to acquire the prior knowledge, skills, and attitudes needed for a given performance task. Teachers have a responsibility to adequately prepare them for the performance task by developing units of study and lessons that will convey the prerequisite knowledge, skills, and work habits all children will need. The new strategies, understandings, and attitudes introduced in the instructional activities should be closely linked to the assessment.

The performance task should appear as a culminating activity in which young people transfer associated knowledge, skills, and work habits from a learning activity to an authentic assessment situation. The task must allow students to demonstrate the understandings and strategies they have learned in a related context without challenging them too much. To meet the individual needs of students, such as second language learners and those with learning disabilities, teachers may have to modify some of the instructional activities.

The Shift Towards Backward Mapping

For some, the move towards authentic assessment and performance-based learning demands a critical shift in pedagogy and curriculum development practices. As the education system changes, assessment becomes a leading force in guiding classroom instruction. The process of backward mapping has become the most innovative strategy in curriculum design. This approach is based on the research of Grant Wiggins and Jay McTighe who wrote *Understanding by Design*, along with the work of educators in Connecticut's Pomeraug Regional School District 15 who wrote *A Teacher's Guide to Performance Based Learning and Assessment*. Planning instruction now begins with establishing focus goals, identifying learning expectations, selecting performance tasks, designing assessment tools, and developing units of study that deliver the content, impart the skills, and instill the work habits required for the culminating activity.

Designing performance tasks can be a challenging endeavour. Valid tasks emerge out of sound curriculum where good instructional activities inform assessment design. The lessons should build the foundation for students' success in the assessment task and aim to improve their overall performance.

Criteria for Instructional Activities That Prepare Students for a Performance Task

- introduce new vocabulary and terms
- build conceptual knowledge and essential understandings
- establish routines and procedures (e.g., following directions)
- teach the safe and proper use of tools, materials, equipment, and resources
- develop and practise important skills and strategies (e.g., reading, mapping, research/inquiry, oral communication)
- provide practical models and examples from real life
- identify basic elements of texts, such as characteristics of a writing form
- introduce different presentation formats (e.g., oral, visual, written) and the methods and techniques used to produce them
- gather, use, and represent information using graphic organizers
- teach higher level thinking skills, including classifying, analyzing, and synthesizing
- analyze patterns, trends, and common features
- encourage a variety of response forms (e.g., the arts)
- provide learning opportunities in pairs, small groups, and whole-class arrangements

Teachers can organize the curriculum for performance learning by developing units of study that focus on conceptual themes (e.g., patterns, relationships); current events; important issues, such as peace; literature; the arts; real-world materials, for example, recipe books, travel brochures, advertising, flyers, and menus; time periods; disciplinary topics (e.g., Science—Weather); and skill development, including higher level thinking.

The Context for Instructional Activities

The instructional activities that appear in this chapter prepare students for the assessment tasks outlined in Chapter 4. Reading the pages consecutively is probably the easiest way to begin. However, if you later choose to adopt a specific assessment unit, you will want to review the overview of assessment units on page 40, where the performance tasks, along with related tools for assessment, data gathering, and reflection, are identified. You can select a task, then locate the instructional activities related to it. When you read the instructional activities featured in this chapter, note "Performance Tasks in Focus," which keys each activity into at least one assessment task.

Based on the curriculum demands and the performance tasks selected, adequate time, learning materials, equipment, and resources need to be arranged. The time allotment may vary according to the class and the students' individual needs. Some lessons may require modifications in order to accommodate learners effectively. Throughout the unit, be sure to track students' progress, using such means as observations and conferences (see Chapter 5), to double-check that students have the foundation required for the assessment. The instructional activities featured in this chapter may provide you with the framework and models for developing innovative lessons, units of study, and performance tasks of your own.

An Overview of Assessment Units

Featured Assessment Unit and Focus Goal	Performance Task/Product	Form of Assessment/ Evaluation	Data Gathering Technique	Reflection Tool
Making Connections with Literature • demonstrate an understanding of reading material and respond to texts using various strategies and formats	Writing a Sequel Oral Retelling	performance assessment lists self-assessment rubric	reading conference question guidelines/ tracking sheets	reading survey
Exploring a Universal Concept: Community • demonstrate an understanding of the concept of community and use subject-specific vocabulary and symbols to communicate information using different presentation tools or writing formats in content areas	Making a Community or Historical Map Scheduling Life in the Community Making Community Goods and Providing Directions Developing a Want Ad	rating scales writing rubric	map observation checklist writing observation checklist	journal writing* performance task questionnaire*
Understanding the Influence of Advertising • interpret and express messages using convincing language and attractive visuals designed to reach and persuade an audience	Developing a Product Creating Body Copy Designing an Ad Layout Packaging a Product	performance checklists oral presentation rubric	rough draft checklist teacher/student/ group questions for conferences; recording and tracking sheets	reflective letter peer conference

* These tools can be used for all assessment units.

Making Connections with Literature

The world of children's literature is an enchanting one filled with fascinating storylines, spectacular settings, dynamic characters, and universal themes that entertain readers of all ages. The rich collection of children's books available today provide young people with a variety of genre and theme selections to choose from and enjoy. Classroom encounters with literature enable readers to enter the story world, understand narrative elements, respond to texts, and develop writing skills in an environment filled with quality publications. Developing a unit of study around children's literature will provide students with an opportunity to strengthen their language skills in meaningful contexts. The instructional activities provided on the following pages have been organized around literacy experiences that will help students understand aspects of story, develop thinking skills, such as making predictions, apply reading strategies, and interact with texts in engaging ways. As young people learn to read, connect, and respond to children's books, they may develop a deep appreciation for literature and a fascination with the story world.

Designing a well-balanced literacy program, filled with rich opportunities to read for enjoyment, for discovery, for enrichment, and for learning, will help nurture a love for reading and interest in books that can last a lifetime.

Working with a Text Set Collection

Performance Tasks in Focus:
Writing a Sequel, Oral Retelling

Task Categories:
reading, locating and gathering information

Materials/Resources:
√ text set collection
√ material for reading log (notebook, paper, folder)

Specific Objectives for Students:

- select and organize reading material for a text set collection based on a particular genre, topic, or theme (A text set collection consists of novels, picture books, short stories, and other works of fiction organized around a common topic or theme.)
- decide on a specific purpose for reading and locate appropriate reading material from a variety of sources
- read independently using a variety of reading strategies

Activity Description:

In order to enrich children's experiences with literature and invite them to enter the story world, try to interest them in the reading material available in the classroom. Begin by selecting a literary genre that children would like to study. Consider, for example, novels, picture books, short stories, myths and legends, fables, folktales, fairy tales, historical or realistic fiction, and science fiction.

You and your class may want to focus your inquiry on a universal theme. You may find themes such as animals, relationships, the past, the future, and the environment interesting.

Topics for literature study may also be generated from work in other curriculum areas. Think of the units investigated in science, social studies, the arts, and other subjects. Many of these can inspire a sense of wonder and motivate young readers to learn more about fascinating topics. Students may want to explore celebrations, immigration, inventions, survival, community living, ecology, habitats, or historical periods, such as pioneer/colonial life or medieval times, for example.

After selecting a genre, theme, or topic of interest, begin creating the text set collection that will be featured in the classroom library. To compose the text set, arrange a visit to the school or local library or bookstore. Enlist the help of the librarian or other staff in locating recent publications of books related to the genre, theme, or topic selected as a class. Be sure to include classic works of fiction in the collection. Use the criteria provided below to make text set selections.

- features works of fiction at different reading levels
- appeals to students' interests and values (contains elements of story that children can relate to)
- allows a variety of interpretations and invites different forms of response
- provides effective models for children's own writing in terms of vocabulary, figurative language, imagery, and so on
- includes multicultural literature written by authors from around the world
- incorporates accurate and relevant information on selected topics
- portrays gender, racial, ethnic, or cultural groups in a positive way (without stereotypes or bias)

Once the literature collection has been compiled, place the books in the classroom library or reading corner. To highlight items in the selection, organize a display on bookshelves and showcases, or arrange the books into bins or baskets according to genre, topic, theme, reading level, or other criterion. Introduce featured books by reading aloud summaries, critical reviews, opening paragraphs/chapters, and interesting parts. Encourage students to add works of literature to the collection whenever they encounter texts related to the selected genre, topic, or theme.

Next, invite the students to select a novel, picture book, short story, or other work of fiction they would like to read. Challenge young people to decide on a specific purpose for reading and to locate a text that meets this goal. Review the different functions of reading with the class, for example, enjoyment and pleasure, information and understanding, vocabulary development, practice and skill improvement (e.g., prediction).

After students have selected a focus and suitable text, allow them to read independently in class. Be sure to model this part of the reading process by choosing a text of your own from the collection. Share the reasons for your selection, and demonstrate effective strategies for reading independently, for example, examining illustrations and rereading passages. Finally, encourage students to develop a reading log, or booklist, outlining the titles of books they have read on their own from the text set collection.

Responding to Reading

Performance Tasks in Focus:
Writing a Sequel, Oral Retelling

Task Categories:
reading, oral
language or communication,
writing, the arts, media literacy

Materials/Resources:
√ reading material (novels, picture books, short stories)
√ reading response log/journal
√ art supplies and materials
√ audio-visual equipment
√ multimedia tools

Specific Objectives for Students:
- respond to texts in a variety of ways that extend their reading experience (These include discussion, writing, and art activities.)
- use their imagination and creativity to respond to reading material

Activity Description:
Young people can develop a greater enjoyment in reading and deeper appreciation for literature by engaging in a variety of response activities. Teachers should provide opportunities for their students to revisit texts through discussion, writing, and art activities that promote higher-level thinking, improve literacy skills and enhance creativity. Many of these response formats have been summarized below.

- *Discussions about Literature:* Encourage students to read and talk about literature with others. These literary conversations may take the form of interviews,

Poster

reading conferences/workshops, book talks, literature circles, class meetings, and panel discussions.

- *Reading Response Log/Journal:* Young people can use reading response logs/journals to make entries based on their literary experiences. They may prepare lists, timelines, jot notes, questions, illustrations, diagrams, or sketches, paragraphs, tables, charts, or webs, maps, personal reactions, and schedules or timetables. These entry formats should enable students to write about literature in a variety of ways, too.
- *Writing Activities:* Encounters with literature may inspire young people to write themselves. After a reading experience, students may interpret story elements from various perspectives and produce writing that can take many text forms. Response writing may include writing-in-role, as in a diary entry, writing a letter, preparing newspaper reports and magazine articles, creating story sequels and additional chapters, offering alternative endings, producing creative spin-offs, providing critical reviews and commentaries, and creating other works of fiction or poetry, for example.
- *Art Experiences:* Readers can enrich their experiences with literature by responding to texts through visual arts, drama, dance, and music. Art activities provide students with opportunities to express their understanding of texts in creative ways. By providing your students with a variety of supplies, materials, tools, props and equipment, you can challenge them to produce powerful and artistic forms of response.
  - visual arts—creating story illustrations, watercolor paintings, papier mâché, collages, posters, 3-D models, dioramas, or murals
  - music—listening to music, singing, writing lyrics, producing song medleys
  - dance—composing dance sequences, moving creatively
  - drama—miming, creating tableaux, improvising, role-playing, writing scripts, doing puppet plays or readers theatre, storytelling, choral reading
- *Audio-visual/Media:* Young people can respond to literature by creating audio-visual productions and multimedia presentations. By providing students with computer and electronic equipment, such as software packages, digital cameras, and other multimedia tools, you can train and challenge readers to produce skillful projects such as

animated comic strips	Internet sites
films or screenplays	video productions
advertisements	television programs or commercials
slideshows	photo essays

In order to support children's language development, it is important to provide them with a variety of opportunities to respond to literature before, during, and after a reading experience. Literary response experiences can take many forms. By selecting activities from the examples provided here or elsewhere, you can enrich students' encounters with texts and deepen their understanding of story.

Read-Aloud Activities

Performance Task in Focus:
Oral Retelling

Task Categories:
reading, oral language or communication, drama

Specific Objectives for Students:
- develop strategies for reading aloud with fluency and expression
- read aloud clearly in a way that communicates meaning
- demonstrate understanding of reading material and awareness of audience while reading aloud

Materials/Resources:
√ Big Books
√ multiple copy texts
√ books at different levels of
  difficulty
√ preselected texts (novels,
  picture books, short stories)
  chosen by the teacher or
  student

Activity Description:

Reading aloud can be a powerful way of experiencing literature. There is no better way to demonstrate the wonderful appeal of a good story than by sharing it with others. It is a good idea to set aside regular periods a day to read aloud to your students, regardless of the grade level you teach. After all, children of all ages enjoy being read to. During these events, model effective strategies for reading aloud. In order to involve students in the experience, select a Big Book to share with the class or distribute copies of the same text for students to use as they listen and read along. Next, read the enlarged book or multiple copy text to the students in an exaggerated way, paying attention to different forms of punctuation. By changing your voice and expression, you can effectively demonstrate how punctuation affects pronunciation. Additional strategies for expressive reading can be modelled to the class by reading aloud dialogue and changing the intonation to show the distinction between the voices of each character and narrator in the story. Provide young readers with practice using these read-aloud techniques by inviting them to read aloud too. After reading a sentence with clarity, fluency, and expression, invite the children to echo the reading or read aloud the text together with you.

Apart from this experience, students can develop effective strategies for reading aloud in other ways. Drama activities can allow them to use some techniques required for oral reading. For instance, students may enjoy presenting a text in a choral performance. During the choral reading, a story can be read in unison, in two-part arrangements, or line by line by different readers, or accompanied by music, sound effects, or movement. During these drama activities, children can develop their read-aloud strategies by revisiting texts with others and presenting story sequences with fluency, clarity, and expression. Changes in voice, volume, and tempo may enhance the oral presentation too.

Another drama and read-aloud event that will enable students to develop their oral reading skills is readers theatre. Here, students select a text to perform for others, highlight the dialogue, appoint individuals to play each character (including a narrator), and practise reading both the narrative and speaking parts aloud before staging the drama simply for others. Entire texts or story excerpts can be carefully prepared for readers theatre by arranging narrative passages and speaking parts into scripts. Since props, costumes, and scenery are often not used during the presentation, readers must interpret story elements and convey meaning to others through the use of voice only. Doing this requires carefully rereading the text and effectively using read-aloud strategies, including punctuation, expression, clarity, and fluency.

Following these events, young people should have opportunities to read aloud to others independently. Begin by having the students select an interesting story they would like to share. Alternatively, choose an appropriate, but unfamiliar text for each student to read aloud. Once the selection is made, introduce or review effective strategies with the class. Encourage readers to use the following techniques during oral reading:

- *background knowledge*, or *schema*, where students use their prior experiences and understandings to make connections with the text
- *sight word recognition*, where students locate known words, such as high-frequency words, that appear in books to help them construct meaning as they read

- *context clues*, where students examine the context in which words are set and use pragmatic cues, such as the organization (structure, features) or information in the text, to help them understand reading material
- *phonetic strategies*, where readers use cueing systems, such as graphophonic cues, to learn about letters, sounds, words, and sentences
- *fluency*, where students develop the rate of their reading by increasing the pace and learning to read faster, more smoothly, and more naturally
- *expression*, where students use oral language and drama techniques, such as changing their voice, regulating the volume, and altering the pitch, during a read aloud
- *clarity*, where students express words clearly as they read by emphasizing certain words or parts
- *punctuation*, where students use punctuation marks in the text as a guide to pause at different points of the reading, such as the end of a sentence

Next, invite students to read to a partner and ask the listener to identify the strategies that the reader used. Later, have children take home a book to read aloud to a parent/guardian and ask adults to note the techniques observed. Review the strategies that others observed in individual readers. Afterwards, schedule time to meet with each student and listen to the child read the selected passage aloud to you. During the read aloud, note the reading strategies being used. In addition to the techniques outlined previously, you may observe reading behaviors such as these:

- finger pointing (tracking words)
- self-correction of miscues
- changing of word endings
- word replacement
- frequent pauses/interruptions
- comprehension
- awareness of audience

By reviewing the data gathered during these oral reading activities, you may learn more about your students' reading strengths and particular difficulties. After recognizing their capacities and weaknesses, you can work together with parents and resource staff to plan learning experiences that will improve each student's ability to read. The goal here remains the same. These learning experiences should help young people develop important language skills and acquire a range of reading strategies they can apply to everyday living, an essential step towards adult literacy.

Elements of Story

Performance Tasks in Focus:
Writing a Sequel, Oral Retelling

Task Categories:
reading, writing, oral language, the arts

Specific Objectives for Students:
- identify basic elements of story—plot, character, setting, theme
- interpret and analyze narrative aspects by responding to texts in a variety of ways (e.g., through discussion, writing, and art activities)
- develop reading, writing, and oral skills by revisiting texts and making meaning in personal and collective ways

Activity Description:
Understanding traditional aspects of literature is an important part of the reading process. Many children's books are filled with compelling storylines, dynamic

Materials/Resources:
√ selected works of children's literature
√ art supplies and materials, including Bristol board and mural paper
√ file/index cards
√ film or digital camera and photo paper
√ costumes and props
√ writing materials (paper, pencil, etc.)

characters, spectacular settings, and powerful themes that command the reader's attention. These elements of fiction often provide open invitations into the story world. By examining narrative aspects in children's literature, young people can develop comprehension skills and recognize essential components that should be included in their own story writing. Studying these traditional elements will provide children with a structural framework to organize and write story sequels and develop their own narratives.

Begin examining the basic elements of story by reading aloud a narrative to the class. Afterwards, ask students to identify the events, characters, settings, and theme in a class discussion. To consolidate children's understanding of these traditional narrative elements, provide opportunities for students to focus on each aspect specifically.

- *Plot:* Ask students to examine the narrative sequence of a story by recalling important incidents at different stages of plot development. Learners can work with others to select opening events, rising actions, turning points, the climax, falling actions, resolutions, and culminating events.

  Next, have students summarize or illustrate critical happenings on file or index cards, posters, collages, or mural paper. Finally, ask learners to arrange the sequence cards, plot summaries, or other demonstrations in order by analyzing the relationship of main events.

- *Character:* Young people can develop an understanding of character by recreating a story as a drama production. To do this, inform the class that auditions and interviews will be held to cast students in the roles of leading characters in a chosen narrative. To earn a role in the drama production, learners must select a character from the narrative and revisit the story to gain information that the author reveals about this person. Prior to the auditions, students can dramatize scenes involving this character and practise speaking parts. Encourage students to assume the role of the character for the auditions by dressing for the part. Following the auditions, ask each student questions that focus on character portrayal, development, and relationships. By responding to the questions in role, young people can reveal aspects of the character's life that may not have been depicted in the audition. After the interview, encourage cast members to rehearse and perform the drama presentation for others. These learning experiences can be extended by having students produce and display cast photos and profiles of story characters appearing in the drama production.

- *Setting:* Invite children to observe the element of setting by revisiting the scenes where the story takes place. Challenge students to note
  - familiar places
  - geographic area, for example, country, city, town, or type of community
  - time period
  - aspects of the physical/natural environment
  - imaginary or other worlds
  - universal locations, such as ocean, lake, or sky
  - interesting landmarks, recreation centres, meeting places
  - places of residence and work/business
  - other important sites

Young readers can form images of the setting by examining any story illustrations and text passages that describe this element in detail. Next, have students select an important story scene and create a diorama, 3-D model, or other physical structure designed to represent the setting.

Postcard

- *Theme:* Students can develop an understanding of the theme in children's literature by staging a debate, talk show, or panel discussion that focuses on this complex element. Prior to the discourse, challenge students to revisit a selected narrative and identify related theme aspects, for example,
  - the central meaning of the story
  - the main idea or topic
  - problems/conflicts addressed in the narrative
  - moral dilemmas and issues raised in the story
  - lessons or universal messages revealed
  - recurring images and symbols

After identifying important concepts related to the theme, students can participate in a formal discussion to analyze and interpret this story element in detail. During the debate, talk show, or panel discussion, young people should raise questions, make judgments, and provide supporting evidence from the text to strengthen their inquiry. Formulating a collective understanding of theme will allow students to develop comprehension strategies and reading skills. In addition to making meaning, they can refine their writing by learning to apply universal themes and complex elements to their own narratives.

By engaging in learning experiences that explore traditional aspects of literature, children's knowledge of narrative structure will grow. Understanding elements of story, and the various techniques used to shape these aspects into a narrative, may assist students with complex tasks, such as demonstrating sequence, oral retelling, developing narratives or extending works of literature that reflect the content and theme of existing texts. Exploring narrative aspects in works of literature will enable young people to develop reading, writing, and oral language skills in a meaningful context based on exemplary models, writing styles, and creative ideas that may be reproduced in children's own writing.

Examining Conflicts

Performance Tasks in Focus:
Writing a Sequel, Oral Retelling

Task Categories:
reading, writing, problem solving

Materials/Resources:
√ picture books, novels, short stories, or other works of fiction
√ literature notebook or reading response log/journal
√ writing supplies and publishing tools, for example, computer

Specific Objectives for Students:
- analyze texts and identify story conflicts
- explain the importance of a story problem and describe its resolution
- provide supportive details and evidence related to the story conflict and resolution from reading material

Activity Description:

Understanding fiction requires the ability to identify narrative aspects and interpret complex story elements. An accomplished author can often maintain the reader's interest by drafting a tale that focuses on characters' problems. Intriguing story conflicts have a way of gripping others through moments of suspense, excitement, anxiety, uncertainty, and relief from the beginning to the final pages of a book. As the resolutions to the problems unfold, the reader is left feeling satisfied or expecting further recourse.

To develop comprehension skills in young readers, provide opportunities for students to analyze story conflicts. Begin by selecting a story that has a clear problem and resolution. Prior to reading the book aloud, ask the children to think about a problem they have experienced and share it with others. Inform the class that they will be listening to a story about a character that has a problem that needs

> Dear Diary,
>   It's me Sarah. Since the time I got here, I feel welcome. The kid's and there father are nice really, but I'am disapointed about leaving Maine. I like it here to but I like the sea much better. My cat is getting along with the dogs but I can tell she misses Maine too. Here in the praires, the fields on the farm look like the sea but not exactly.

Sample diary letter

> Dear Sarah Elisabeth Wheaton
>   I am Jacob witting, I am answering your letter. Yes you may take care of my children. Their names are Caleb and Anna. I will tell you all about me, and my children. I will tell you all about where I live. I am glad that you are interested in my children. Do you do work like cooking, cleaning, laundry and other house work? No I don't live near the sea. No I don't have a cat.
>   Your truly,
>   Jacob witting

Sample letter

Performance Task in Focus:
Writing a Sequel

Task Categories:
reading, oral language, writing

Materials/Resources:
√ picture books, novels, short stories with a predictable plot or patterned sequence

to be solved. During the read aloud, listeners should consider the important problem in the story, reflect on its importance, and recall the resolution reached at the end of the book. Following the story, invite learners to share their interpretations and recollections with the class. To facilitate analysis of the story problem, have all the children focus on the same problem initially. For books with complex plots and several characters, teachers and students need to determine beforehand the character whose problem will be analyzed. As a large group, summarize the major conflicts in the story and identify the main problems faced by the selected character. Once these have been identified, have students explain why the character's problem is important in relation to plot developments and the actions of other characters. Finally, ask learners to explain how the conflict was resolved. As a class, select one of these writing activities to use as a response:

- diary entry
- letter to a character
- advice column (letter seeking advice and expert response)

Next, draft a copy of the diary entry, letter, or advice column with the students, including supportive details and information from the story.

To develop students' ability to interpret and analyze story conflicts and resolutions independently, invite children to make their own book selections and read the texts quietly. During the reading experience, encourage learners to note the character, problem, importance, and resolution in a response log or literature notebook. To consolidate this skill, you may challenge students to examine several characters simultaneously and interpret major conflicts and secondary problems too. In response, have readers select one of the writing activities noted above. In order to ensure that the written response indicates the child's comprehension of the story, remind the students to include facts, examples, and details from the narrative to support their interpretations. Finally, invite learners to publish their letters or diary entries and share their work with others. These engaging experiences, along with other reading activities, will enable students to process, analyze, and understand complex information in critical and thoughtful ways.

Making Predictions

Specific Objectives for Students:

- develop reading strategies (rereading, predicting content, etc.) that assist with comprehension
- analyze texts and make predictions
- provide reasons and evidence to support their predictions

Activity Description:

Throughout their reading, students should be encouraged to examine story elements and forecast events. The ability to make predictions is an important skill that all readers should develop. To facilitate this, select an interesting narrative to read aloud to the class. An appealing story that causes reaction and invites projection would make an effective choice. Depending on the age/grade level of your students, you may select an appropriate text from a range of reading materials to share with children during a read-aloud event. For example:

- pattern stories
- rhyming texts

Predicting: I think that Sarah will be very happy when she comes to visit. I think that she will like the children and the father. I think she will feel happy about living on a farm. Sarah will teach the children how to sing. They could spend their time together by Sarah telling everyone about her life. I think Sarah will stay at their house.

Sample prediction about *Sarah, Plain and Tall*

• books with rhythmic language and repetitive refrains (notably Dr. Seuss)
• series books, such as Harry Potter or Adventures in Narnia
• sequels/chronological texts
• books written by the same author, perhaps Eric Carle or Chris Van Allsburg

Prior to reading aloud, engage your students in a discussion about the text by reviewing such features as the book jacket/cover, the information provided about the author and illustrator, and possibly book reviews. Next, discuss the title and examine the cover illustration for clues about the story. Invite students to make predictions and relate personal experiences.

Following the discussion, begin reading the story aloud to the class. Throughout this experience, interrupt the reading to allow students to make predictions and forecast events and character actions. You may decide on effective places to stop reading aloud prior to sharing the story and mark text passages that cause reaction, invite response, and include anticipated elements. At selected points of the story, have students suggest possible words, repetitive language, probable actions, subsequent episodes, pending dialogue, and logical resolutions.

It is important to provide listeners with sufficient information about the characters and the story problem before asking them to make predictions. Demonstrate your own ability to predict story outcomes by reading aloud to the class, stopping at opportune times to make predictions, and offering reasons for your projections based on narrative information already read. After encountering parts of the story that reveal the accuracy of any prediction, confirm your ideas with the class, or alter your projections based on new evidence. Doing this will provide an effective model for students making their own predictions.

You may initially use a questioning strategy that encourages students to make predictions. In addition to helping children forecast events, these questions should challenge them to revisit prior projections and confirm or revise their predictions. As part of the process, students should be required to support their predictions with evidence, namely, facts, examples, and details from the text, or share related personal experiences. Questions that would encourage these reading behaviors and promote higher-level thinking include these:

What do you think will happen next? What makes you think this?
What do you think [the character] might do? Why? What makes you think this?
Were your predictions about the story correct?
How would you change your predictions based on new information you have learned?

Following the read-aloud event, let children reflect on the story and respond to the narrative. To hone their ability to make predictions, students can construct a new beginning or preceding episode, or craft a new ending or succeeding episode with others. Working with peers during the writing activity will enable young people to use their collective imagination and understanding of story details to produce a logical addition to the text. These learning experiences will promote important reading skills, like making predictions, which is an essential part of constructing meaning and developing critical thinking.

Story Mapping and Storytelling

Performance Tasks in Focus:
Oral Retelling, Writing a Sequel

Task Categories:
reading, the arts, oral language,
cooperative learning

Materials/Resources:
√ picture books, short stories,
  novels and other works of
  fiction
√ storytelling aids and props
  (e.g., feltboard cutouts)
√ visual art supplies and materials

Specific Objectives for Students:
• develop reading skills, such as sequencing
• identify and present story elements in different formats, including visually
• produce story maps and use storytelling aids and props to present narratives

Activity Description:

Recognizing the narrative sequence of a story is an important skill that young people need to develop in order to understand literature and write well. You can provide opportunities for students to examine plotlines and other story elements in many creative ways. Begin by selecting an interesting book to read aloud to the class. An appealing narrative filled with compelling characters, exciting events, and dynamic settings would make a good selection.

Prior to reading aloud, present students with a logical framework to interpret story events. One option would be to provide listeners with a chart, or table, similar to the one below, that can be used to select and interpret the narrative sequence:

Beginning	Middle	Ending

Alternatively, teachers may use a questioning strategy to assist students in understanding literary texts. In addition to focusing on storyline, these prompts can address other important narrative aspects. Present listeners with a series of focus questions to guide them through the read-aloud event. For example:

How did the story begin?	How is the conflict/problem solved?
Who is the story about?	Who is part of the resolution?
What happens in the story?	How does the story end?
What is the conflict/problem?	What is the order of events in the story?

Another method that can be used to develop students' understanding of plot and other narrative elements is a recording sheet featuring headings that outline important aspects of the story. Listeners can note aspects during or following the read-aloud event. A sample recording sheet is provided on the next page.

After providing the students with these frameworks, read the story to the class for enjoyment and pleasure. Then, during a second reading, encourage listeners to

• use their imaginations to visualize narrative aspects described by the author
• produce sketches of important story elements
• consider the focus questions raised previously and record/discuss related content
• note important information on a graphic organizer or recording sheet

To develop a collective understanding of the narrative sequence and other story aspects, organize the class into cooperative learning groups and assign each group a different section of the text to recreate artistically. Learners can interpret events and portray settings, characters, and important episodes by designing a mural,

Reading Recording Sheet

Title of the Story:

_____

Author:

_____

Setting:

_____

_____

Main Characters:

_____

_____

_____

_____

Story Problem/Conflict:

_____

_____

_____

_____

_____

Important Episodes and Major Events

1._____

_____

2._____

_____

3._____

_____

4._____

_____

5._____

_____

Solution:

_____

_____

Overall Lesson or Theme:

_____

_____

_____

_____

© 2003 *Authentic Assessment* by Katherine Luongo-Orlando. Pembroke Publishers. All rights reserved. Permission to reproduce for classroom use.

collage, diorama, or other visual demonstration. Later, the class can arrange the sections in logical progression as each group retells story events in order.

To prepare students for their own retelling, guide children through story selection in order to ensure that each learner makes an appropriate choice. Once students have found a story to share with others, they should be encouraged to read it several times independently. After becoming familiar with a narrative, students can produce a story map to assist in the retelling. This graphic tool can take many visual formats, including story webs, storyboards, and story cards, as illustrated on the following page.

After recording, illustrating, and arranging story elements (characters, setting, problems, events) in sequence using a story mapping model they are comfortable with, students can use the graphic tool they created to retell their story to others. The retelling experience can be enriched by the use of props—feltboards and cutouts, for example, to represent narrative aspects too.

Written Retellings, Oral Recordings, and Transcripts

Performance Task in Focus:
Oral Retelling

Task Categories:
reading, writing, oral language

Materials/Resources:
√ selected literature resources suited for retelling
√ reading log, literature book, or response journal
√ cassette tapes and recorders

Specific Objectives for Students:
• develop reading strategies and oral language techniques
• describe elements of story in written and oral recounts
• retell a story by adapting it for presentation in another way (e.g., as a written recount, oral recording, or transcript)

Activity Description:

Children are natural storytellers who enjoy the excitement, creativity, and fun of listening to and telling stories. Retellings come easily to young people because they genuinely love to share tales they have read or heard. A retelling is an oral or written recounting of a story in a child's own words. Developing a recount usually requires a child to identify important story elements and use a variety of language skills.

Young people can be provided with a range of retelling experiences in the classroom and beyond. *Unguided* retellings are those where students retell spontaneously and share story elements openly without intervention. *Guided* retellings are those where students are prompted to retell with support. Here, focus questions, response cues, or other strategies are used to encourage participation or provide direction when students are having difficulty recalling information and retelling story parts on their own.

As teachers begin to use retellings as an assessment tool, it is important to provide students with effective models and balanced approaches that will refine children's natural ability to tell stories.

To begin, gather books that have strong structures and elements of story. Select a narrative to share with the class and read the text aloud to the students. Following the read aloud, retell the story to the group using a variety of techniques to convey meaning and entertain listeners. Effective strategies may include

• using selected phrases from the text
• pausing for effect
• altering the pitch or tone
• emphasizing certain words or parts
• regulating the volume
• changing the pace

Story Mapping

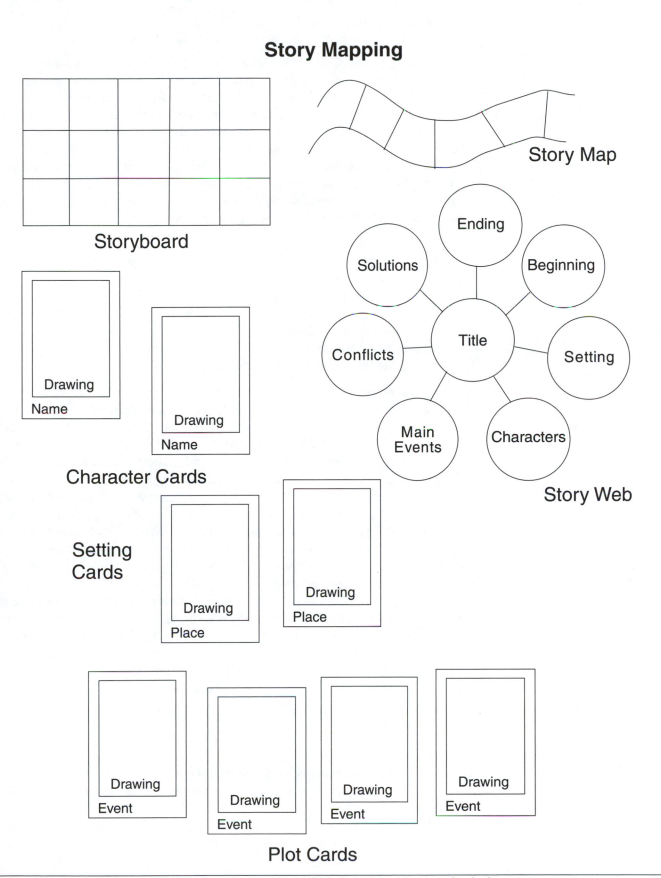

Storyboard

Story Map

Character Cards

Drawing
Name

Drawing
Name

Story Web

Ending

Solutions

Beginning

Conflicts

Title

Setting

Main Events

Characters

Setting Cards

Drawing
Place

Drawing
Place

Drawing
Event

Drawing
Event

Drawing
Event

Drawing
Event

Plot Cards

© 2003 *Authentic Assessment* by Katherine Luongo-Orlando. Pembroke Publishers. All rights reserved. Permission to reproduce for classroom use.

- modifying voice for variety
- using text illustrations as a guide
- introducing props or symbols

Throughout the retelling, encourage students to close their eyes and visualize the story. After all, making pictures in one's mind is a useful reading strategy.

After modelling the retelling process for the class, invite students to select a narrative to share with others and read it independently. Then, encourage learners to tell the story to a peer who hasn't read it yet. To develop this skill further, ask students to produce a written retelling, or recount, of the narrative. Young people can record written retellings in a reading log, literature book, or response journal. Encourage students to revisit the story and recall information they can include in their recounts. Provide students with these prompts for eliciting specific story elements and details that should be noted in their retellings:

- Where does the story take place? When?
- Who is the main character in the story? Who are the other characters?
- How does the story begin?
- What is the important problem in the story?
- What events happen in the story? What is the order of these events?
- How is the problem solved?
- How does the story end?
- What is the theme or message of the story?

After students have produced a written retelling, ask them to record it on cassette tape without referring to the text or their written retelling. Have learners play back the recording for peers, parents, volunteers, and others and note the effective strategies used and story elements included. In a reflective discussion, challenge students to identify areas for improvement (e.g., additional content and techniques to be developed). Encourage students to practise and refine their retellings. Later, ask parents, volunteers, teacher aides, or older students to transcribe the material on tape by recording words exactly as students have produced them. Transcripts of the oral retelling should be dated and included in student portfolios for ongoing observation and assessment purposes. Reading transcripts (or listening to the tape) can provide you with important information about children's comprehension and reading skills.

The ability to share stories with others has the power to evolve into a creative art form. In storytelling, the art occurs in the presentation. Becoming an effective storyteller requires practice in listening, reading, writing, and speaking, essential components in language development. By engaging in learning experiences that focus on the task of retelling, young people will be able to refine communication skills that can be used in the classroom and the real world.

Story Dialogue

Performance Task in Focus:
Writing a Sequel

Task Categories:
reading, writing, oral language, drama

Specific Objectives for Students:
- examine the role of dialogue in children's literature
- adapt and reconstruct texts by presenting them in another way (e.g., as a script, dramatization)
- develop drama techniques and oral language skills by recreating, improvising, and/or role-playing story dialogue with others

Activity Description:

Read aloud to the class a picture book, short story, novel chapter, or other narrative that includes conversations between characters. Examine the place of dialogue in the story. Many authors begin their writing in the middle of an episode where characters are already immersed in conversation. Apart from introducing the scene, story dialogue can appear throughout a text and facilitate plot development.

As a class, revisit the literary conversations in a text and generate a list of ways that dialogue can enrich the story and enhance comprehension. For example, literary conversations can provide deeper insight into a character (interior monologue), build understanding of character relationships, foreshadow upcoming events, and offer different interpretations of or perspectives on narrative elements.

Once students have examined the information divulged in literary discourse, ask them to use the models found in children's books to determine the features of story dialogue. They will likely find active words, relevant content, vocabulary that reflects characters' age, role in the story, and so on, an authentic sense of voice, typical patterns of human speech, for example, nuances, sighs, interruptions, and grammatical errors, and specific writing format and structure (capitalization, quotation marks, etc.).

Next, have students select dialogue from a story they are interested in and reconstruct it into a screenplay, adapted for performance. After producing a script of the interactive text, learners can assign roles, practise speaking parts, and present their dramatizations to others as readers theatre.

In addition, students can work in pairs or small groups to compose a dialogue for a picture book, short story, or other work of literature that does not contain conversations between characters. Learners may role-play these interactions before producing the written discourse.

For further practice, students can improvise chance encounters between characters from different children's books and present the literary exchange as a comic strip using talk bubbles or dialogue balloons.

Once young writers begin including dialogue in their narratives and experimenting with quotation marks, offer additional strategies and support for mastering this sophisticated tool. Lists of rules for using dialogue, quotation marks, and other technical components would be helpful.

The learning experiences provided here will help young readers and writers develop comprehension strategies, improve oral language skills, refine story writing, and include a natural form of communication into their work.

Examining Authors' Use of Style

Specific Objectives for Students:

- develop their vocabulary by reading a variety of children's books
- examine the language and style of writing in works of children's literature
- identify elements of distinctive writing, such as imagery, stylistic devices, and connecting words

Activity Description:

Authors of children's literature can provide young people with exemplary models for writing their own narratives. By examining the works of talented writers, young people can be inspired to create their own story books. Works of literature

---

Materials/Resources:

√ picture books, short stories, novels, and other narratives that include dialogue
√ chart paper, markers
√ pens/pencils and paper

Performance Task in Focus:
Writing a Sequel

Task Categories:
reading, writing

Materials/Resources:

√ art supplies and materials
√ exemplary works of children's literature* (see page 58)
√ Handout: "Exploring the Writer's Craft" (see page 57)

The List of Similes.

Mieko felt the bitterness inside of her beginning to disappear like the early morning mist. (pg 48) Compares herself to the weather. √

She felt like a small child learning to write for the first time. (pg 48) Compares herself to a small child. √

"You girls are as close as a pair of chopsticks." (pg 49) Yoshi and Mieko being compared to chopsticks. √

Sample list of similes from *Mieko and the Fifth Treasure*, Chapter 7

written for children can provide aspiring young writers with ideas, style, and language to use in their own work.

Begin examining the language of the text, style of writing, author's use of voice, and imaginary and literary devices by selecting exemplary works from children's literature. Provide models from a range of genres—novels, short stories, picture books, poems. Read aloud to the class passages that demonstrate the elements of distinctive writing. Focus on style, form, structure, and diction by examining the way the writer uses effective vocabulary, sentence structure, imagery, and language devices to communicate ideas, engage the imagination, invoke responses, establish meaning, and convey messages. Introduce, define, and provide examples of stylistic devices, such as allusion, simile, metaphor, personification, and symbolism. Record and display selected phrases, descriptions, and expressions written by talented children's authors in favorite books or exemplary works of literature.

Provide opportunities for students to examine the diction and figurative language that authors use to produce a distinctive effect in their writing. Challenge learners to locate examples of stylistic devices in children's books. Encourage students to develop their vocabulary by producing lists of the following:

- similes, metaphors, examples of personification, and other literary tools
- words that link ideas in or between paragraphs
  (e.g., *also, finally, but, although, in addition*)
- transition words/phrases that show the passage of time
  (e.g., *next, later, suddenly, soon after, the following day*)
- words that create mood
- diverse verbs for writing story dialogue
  (e.g., *asked, replied, exclaimed, explained, answered, mentioned* instead of *said*)
- descriptive passages that create powerful images
- text selections that arouse emotions
- expressions and figures of speech

Students can develop reference lists on recording sheets, like the one provided on the next page.

After examining the style and language of children's books, students can apply their literary knowledge in a range of learning experiences. As a whole class, they could create a graffiti wall, where they can use art supplies and writing tools to graphically present words and phrases from children's books for others to read. Encourage them to use the language phrases and literary tools taken from literature in their own creative writing. Challenge them to use figurative language, literary devices, and expressions found in books to create poems, song lyrics, and media works, such as slogans and jingles, by arranging and combining selected words and phrases together. They can also compile expressions, figures of speech, and stylistic devices found in children's literature with the intent of producing writing resources. These resource books, with titles such as A Dictionary of Similes, An Alphabet Book of Story Symbols, A Pocket Guide to Using Personification, and The Meaning and Origin of Popular Expressions, can be published and made available at a writing centre for reference purposes throughout the year. Finally, students can revisit descriptive text passages that use imagery and draw or paint a picture or create a work of art that depicts the powerful image the words create.

By providing students with enriching learning experiences that enable them to explore an author's use of words, writing style, and language form, young people will be able to develop their vocabulary and refine their writing skills as they learn the writer's craft and apply it to their own narratives.

Exploring the Writer's Craft

Select several works of children's literature, including picture books, novels, and short stories. Carefully read and examine the language forms, writing tools, and vocabulary used by different authors. Record examples in the spaces below. (*Optional:* Note the title of the book and page number where each example can be found.)

**Stylistic devices
(similes, metaphors, etc.)**

Other words for *Said*

_____

_____

_____

_____

_____

Words that create mood

Words that awaken feelings

_____

_____

_____

_____

_____

Connecting or linking words

**Transition words/Phrases
that show the passage of time**

_____

_____

_____

_____

_____

Descriptive passages that use imagery

Expressions/Figures of speech

_____

_____

_____

_____

_____

© 2003 *Authentic Assessment* by Katherine Luongo-Orlando. Pembroke Publishers. All rights reserved. Permission to reproduce for classroom use.

*See the following resource books for suggested reading lists that will assist with quality literature selections:

Best Books for Kids Who Think They Hate to Read: 125 Books That Will Turn Any Child into a Lifelong Reader by Laura Backes
Reading and Writing in the Middle Years by David Booth
Better Books! Better Readers! How to Choose, Use and Level Books in the Primary Grades by Linda Hart-Hewins and Jan Wells
Children's Literature in the Elementary School, 7th Edition, by Charlotte S. Huck, Susan Hepler, Janet Hickman, and Barbara Z. Kiefer
Beyond Leveled Books: Supporting Transitional Readers in Grades 2–5 by Karen Szymusiak and Franki Sibberson

Exploring a Universal Concept: Community

Living in the world today challenges us to reach beyond the limits of our own society and neighborhoods, and embrace a universe filled with many people, places, and cultures. Global boundaries that once separated us from others seem to be fading. Children of our generation are growing up in a world that is becoming smaller with each innovation in information technology.

Helping young people understand the commonality of our experiences and the universal concept of community can be challenging when all they know and envision is their home and immediate environment. Developing a unit of study around the idea of community may enable students to understand important features and aspects of living in a global village. The instructional activities provided on the following pages have been developed with this universal concept in mind. Learning about community living challenges students to formulate and apply many skills. The ability to use specialized vocabulary, symbols, presentation tools, and writing formats are important strengths for young people to have. To help students develop the language methods and communication systems required to function in this period of rapid global change, authentic learning experiences need to be provided. When these opportunities are provided in an environment supported by a sense of community, a state of global awareness can emerge. Suddenly, the communication methods used have the power to cross boundaries and reach people around the world who share our environment and our humanity.

Community Concepts

Performance Tasks in Focus:
Making a Community or Historical Map, Developing a Want Ad, Scheduling Life in the Community, Making Community Goods and Providing Directions

Task Categories:
building concepts and vocabulary, organizing information

Specific Objectives for Students:
• describe the major features of a community
• identify characteristics of urban and rural communities
• record and classify information on charts and graphic organizers

Activity Description:

As a class, discuss the term *community*. Invite students to share their ideas on the meaning of this word. Create a word web that includes the specific features and definitions students generated.

Next, have students identify the characteristics of urban and rural communities. Begin by displaying pictures from travel brochures, magazines, newspapers, reference books, and other sources that feature these community types. In pairs or

Materials/Resources:
√ chart paper
√ markers
√ pictures of urban and rural
  communities, perhaps from
  travel brochures, magazines,
  newspapers, or reference books

small groups, have students record and classify information on a T-table, similar to the one below:

T-TABLE

Urban	Rural
residential	fishing
business	farming
industrial	forestry
commercial	mining

As a class, produce a general list of communities from around the world throughout history. These might include early/ancient civilizations, medieval society, pioneer/colonial life, tribes of Aboriginal peoples, and the local community.

As a challenge, invite the students to list the communities identified in chronological order and record them on a timeline.

Finally, select a topic for the unit of study by focusing on a particular community in either the past or the present that will be investigated as a class. In small or large groups, have students fill in a K-W-L chart, like the one below.

K-W-L CHART

What I Know	What I Want to Know	What I Learned

Developed by Donna Ogle

Afterwards, invite learners to share their background knowledge of the topic, their interests, and research questions prior to further inquiry.

Creating a Picture Dictionary

Specific Objectives for Students:

• develop and use subject-specific vocabulary to communicate information
• use a dictionary and thesaurus to expand vocabulary

Performance Tasks in Focus:
Making Community Goods and
Providing Directions, Scheduling
Life in the Community, Making a
Community or Historical Map,
Developing a Want Ad

Task Category:
building concepts and vocabulary

Activity Description:

As a class, brainstorm words related to the community, time period, or unit you are studying. Have students refer to resource/trade books and literature sources such as picture books, and novels dealing with these topics and identify new vocabulary encountered in these texts. Be sure to compile an alphabetical list of unknown terms (a variety of words beginning with the same letter may be featured in this list). Here are some sample vocabulary lists:

Materials/Resources:

√ writing tools, including paper, colored pencils, and computer equipment
√ dictionary
√ thesaurus
√ resource/trade books
√ literature

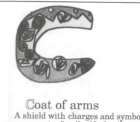

Coat of arms
A shield with charges and symbols that represent a family. No family can have the same shield.

Queen- a member of the royal family who rules over a kingdom

Performance Tasks in Focus:
Making a Community or Historical Map, Developing a Want Ad

Task Category:
organizing information

Materials/Resources:

√ resource materials
√ graphic organizer handout, "The Parts of a Community"
√ K-W-L chart (see page 59)

TYPE OF COMMUNITY

Local	Pioneer	Medieval
arena	artisan	chain mail
butcher shop	barter system	duke
community centre	blacksmith	estate
dwelling	crock	feudal system
...	dam	guild
landmark	embroidery	herald
...	flog	illumination
shelter	harness	joust
silos	jackstraws ...	keep ...

After compiling a comprehensive list of new vocabulary words, have students select a word they want to investigate. Prior to their investigations, introduce or review important vocabulary-building resources, such as a dictionary, a thesaurus, a glossary, and an index. Teach students how to locate vocabulary words from these resources. Following alphabetical order and guide words are examples.

After students understand their selected word, challenge them to define it in their own words. Remind learners to use language that both their peers and younger children will understand. Have students create an illustration to match the definition they have written. As an option, learners can publish their word, definitions, and illustrations on the computer. Final copies of all the vocabulary pages can then be compiled and arranged alphabetically to form a picture dictionary. Once the book has been bound together, it can be displayed and used for reference purposes. You could also encourage students to use a variety of presentation tools and art techniques (e.g., drama, computer slide show, visual arts display) to communicate their findings to the class. That will allow others to become familiar with words they may encounter throughout the unit.

Determining What Makes a Community Unique

Specific Objectives for Students:

• identify the distinguishing features of a community
• sort, classify, and record information on charts and graphic organizers

Activity Description:

As a class, take a walk in the local community, noting important characteristics. Have students investigate aspects of the community they are studying in reference books and other resource materials, such as CD-ROMs and Web sites. Ask learners to complete the handout "The Parts of a Community" by noting information related to the topic, unit, and time period they are studying. They may work individually, in pairs or in small groups. As a class, discuss the distinguishing features of community being investigated. Have students use the results of their inquiry to fill in the K-W-L chart appropriately.

The Parts of a Community

TOPIC/UNIT/TIME PERIOD:

Places (e.g., buildings)	People

Transportation Methods	Physical Features (landforms, natural resources)

© 2003 *Authentic Assessment* by Katherine Luongo-Orlando. Pembroke Publishers. All rights reserved. Permission to reproduce for classroom use.

Exploring a Community Through Maps

Performance Task in Focus:
Making a Community or
Historical Map

Task Categories:
reading maps, locating
information, developing mapping
skills

Materials/Resources:
√ a map of the school
√ a variety of specific maps (e.g.,
   building, amusement park, and
   road)
√ a collection of maps on
   different communities, ranging
   from local and rural to urban,
   country, or world

Specific Objectives for Students:
• read and locate information from a map
• identify symbols used to mark locations and features on a map
• learn to consult map legends when locating specific features on a map

Activity Description:

As a class, collect and display a variety of maps. Identify the common features, such as title, symbols, cardinal directions, legend, and scale.

Next, examine maps or floor plans of the school. Have students locate familiar places, such as the office and library, and identify the symbols used to mark their location. Ask learners to note important routes within the school (e.g., fire route) featured on the map.

Later, have students examine community maps and identify the symbols used to mark general features and landmarks, such as roads, railway crossings, hospitals, other important buildings (e.g., the fire or police station), homes and dwellings, and waterways. Produce a list of these pictorial symbols that can be used as reference.

Display a map that features a legend. Demonstrate how the legend is used to locate information on the map. Review the symbols included on the legend. Have students refer to the legend to find specific features on the map. Finally, provide students with an opportunity to work with others to read maps and locate information by consulting a legend.

Making Maps of a Community

Performance Task in Focus:
Making a Community or
Historical Map

Task Categories:
developing mapping skills,
producing maps, labelling
information

Materials/Resources:
√ a variety of maps
√ mapping tools (e.g., rulers,
   colored pencils, and paper)

Specific Objectives for Students:
• produce maps and label important features
• use symbols, color, and cardinal directions on a map
• construct map legends with pictorial symbols that represent landmarks

Activity Description:

Invite students to recount their trip to school using familiar landmarks and places in their local community to describe their route. As a class, produce a list of local landmarks and prominent features in the community. These may include apartment buildings, the fire station, the police station, a hospital, crosswalk for a busy street, a recreation centre, a public library, local business and a park/playground.

Review the list of pictorial symbols used to identify common landmarks (e.g., H for hospital) on maps and map legends. Consult other map legends, or develop your own symbols to represent specific features found in the school community. As a class, begin constructing a map of the local community by producing a legend and using pictorial symbols to represent significant landmarks. Invite students to recreate familiar buildings, places, and areas of their community on different sections of the map. Challenge them to complete the map individually, in pairs, in small groups, or as a class.

Afterwards, examine a variety of maps that use color and cardinal directions (North, South, East, West). Assist students in recognizing that different colors on maps indicate or represent different features: for example, blue is used for rivers and waterways; countries appear in different colors to denote size and boundaries. Challenge students to describe locations on a map using cardinal directions. Ask learners to include cardinal directions on the map of their local community. Have students color the map they produced appropriately.

For additional practice, students can produce maps of the classroom and label important features. Have learners compare and contrast the maps they made by identifying similar characteristics and mapping techniques. In order to consolidate their mapping skills, learners can produce a map of their home using symbols, colors, labels, and other important features covered in this lesson.

Exploring the World of Work

Performance Tasks in Focus:
Developing a Want Ad, Scheduling Life in the Community

Task Categories:
writing, drama, role playing

Materials/Resources:
√ newspaper
√ journal

Specific Objectives for Students:
• identify the occupations of members of the community
• describe the roles and responsibilities of people in the community
• represent people in the community by speaking and writing-in-role

Activity Description:
Have students examine the want ads found in the Classified sections of local newspapers and note important features such as job description; required skills, education, and experience; important duties and responsibilities of the job; and the application process.

Next, ask learners to investigate and produce a list of occupations held by members of the community they are studying. Here are some sample lists:

Local	Pioneer	Medieval
storekeeper	farmer	squire/page/knight
mail carrier	harness maker	herald
teacher	carpenter	lady-in-waiting
police officer	blacksmith	steward
doctor	cobbler	minstrel
firefighter	wheelwright	stone mason
secretary	cooper	falconer
bus driver	printer	troubadour
farmer	bookbinder	jester
nurse	paper maker	guard

Classified Ad

Hear ye hear ye

The king needs a knight. The knight will be required to guard the castle from the gatehouse to fight in wars when needed, and to protect the king, queen and the other members of the royal family. The knight will receive three meals a day, five gold coins a week and a place to stay in the castle. If interested report to the castle tomorrow at noon.

Encourage students to explore this important aspect of community life through drama. Ask each learner, working with a partner, to assume the role of either an employer or a job applicant. Invite the job applicant to select an occupation from the list he or she may be interested in. Before applying for the job posting, have the job applicant note relevant skills, education, and experience that make him or her suitable for the job. Meanwhile, ask the employer to produce a list of interview questions and identify the specific duties and responsibilities of the job. Later, have each pair role-play the job interview and improvise the conversation that takes place. Then, repeat the drama scenario by having students switch roles. Finally, challenge students to write a journal entry in role, where they describe a job in the community they are studying from the first-person point of view.

Exploring Daily Life Through Schedules

Developing a Want Ad,
Scheduling Life in the
Community

Task Categories:
developing research skills,
organizing information

Materials/Resources:
√ daily timetables, schedules
√ resource materials
√ literature collections
√ excerpt from a novel, picture
  book, or short story
√ primary document, for
  example, a copy of an original
  letter, journal entry, list, or
  diary

Specific Objectives for Students:
• describe the duties and responsibilities of people in their everyday life
• begin to develop research skills

Activity Description:

In a large group, review the daily schedule or class timetable, noting important features such as time periods, subjects, events, and activities. Ask students to collect examples of other lists, schedules, timetables, and planning charts. These might include a Things To Do list; sports schedule for practices, games, and tournaments; work schedule, and travel itinerary. Have learners examine the format and organization of these planning frameworks and identify common features, including

• specified time slots/periods
• list of activities
• task descriptions
• ordered sequence of events
• arrangement/layout, as in a chart, list, or table

As a class, discuss the duties and responsibilities of students' family members. Read an excerpt from a novel, picture book, short story, or other text that describes the daily tasks and chores of people in the community and time period being studied. Share a copy of an original letter, journal entry, list, or other primary document that describes the everyday life and work of a member of the community. Discuss the roles and responsibilities of people in their everyday life.

In groups, have students examine the roles of community members and identify their specific responsibilities using resource books and other reference materials. Ask learners to record their findings on a chart similar to the one below:

Daily Chores, Duties, and Responsibilities

Men	Women	Children

6:00am Eat Breakfast
6:30am Get dressed for Work
7:00am Gather farming tools
7:30am Go to Garden.
8:00am Milk Cows
8:30   Gather eggs from chickens
8:45   Feed geese or goose
9:00   Milk goats
9:30   Work in carrot gardens.
10:30   Collect herbs and spices.
11:00am Cook lunch (fish, rice)
11:30   Eat lunch
12:00   Go back to Work
12:30   Clean hut.
1:00pm Go to potato Garden
2:00pm Rest - Listen to stories, sing songs. etc.
2:30pm Go fetch Water (for drinking)
3:15pm Plough Fields.
3:45pm Go fishing at the pond.
4:00pm Feed all the animals
5:00   Water all plants.
6:30   Go home
6:00   Cook dinner (steak, rice & pumpkin pie)
7:00   Get prepared for bed.

Schedule for peasant girl

Later, encourage students to share their findings with others.

Examining Instructions for Making Community Goods

Performance Task in Focus:
Making Community Goods and
Providing Directions

Task Categories:
following instructions, developing
research skills, writing

Materials/Resources:
√ artifact, craft good, or food
  item
√ arts and crafts supplies
√ bowls and containers (wooden
  and cardboard boxes)
√ stove, if recipe requires
√ cooking utensils and
  ingredients
√ recipes and instructions, as in
  resource books and newspapers

How to Dye Clothes

Materials
Plants
Large pots filled with water
Logs for fire
Mordant (large spoon)

Instructions
1. Gather plants that have lots of colour.
2. Get a large pot and fill with water.
3. Put plant leaves in the water to get all the colour out.
4. Use the logs to make a small fire.
5. Put pot over the fire.
6. Then stir with mordant and wait.
7. Add fabric or clothing to the coloured water and let sit.
8. Remove fabric or clothing from water and let dry.
9. Sew fabric into clothing or wear dyed clothes.

Performance Tasks in Focus:
Making Community Goods and
Providing Directions, Scheduling
Life in the Community

Task Categories:
developing research skills,
developing writing
skills—exploring text forms,
planning events

Specific Objectives for Students:
- identify important aspects of community living
- read instructions and follow procedures carefully in sequence

Activity Description:

Display an artifact, craft good, or food item that reflects the type of community and time period being studied. Examples include quilt, tapestry, cooking utensil, or baked good. As a class, discuss how the displayed object represents important aspects of community living and everyday life.

Ask students to collect recipes, instructions on how to make craft objects, and other forms of procedural writing ranging from game instructions to user manuals related to the topic. Have them examine the format, language, and organization of this text form and produce a list of common features. They will probably note

- framework headings: ingredients, materials, equipment/utensils/tools, directions/instructions, and method
- connecting words: *first, then, after, when, once,* etc.
- factual details, information, and descriptions (e.g., type and quantity of materials, time requirements, precise measurements)
- step-by-step guidelines/procedures presented in ordered sequence
- diagrams, photographs, or labelled drawings

As a class, select a recipe for a food item from the community being studied. Gather the required ingredients, utensils, and materials. Display a copy of the recipe for students to read. Invite student volunteers to follow each step or procedure in sequence. Once the recipe is complete, have students sample the food they made.

In small or large groups, ask students to produce a list of foods, craft objects, cultural artifacts, and others goods that reflect the community being investigated. Encourage learners to use a variety of resource materials and research methods to compile their lists. Some featured items may include traditional dishes; baked goods; preserved foods, such as jam; household items, for example, soap and candles; handmade objects, such as pottery, quilts, and tapestries; daily chores; home remedies for common illnesses; tools and utensils; and toys and games.

Invite each student to select an object from the list that he or she would like to learn more about. Have learners research the origins and construction of their objects, produce drawings or illustrations of them, and write brief summaries or descriptions that might appear in a catalogue or museum exhibit.

Researching Recreational Activities

Specific Objectives for Students:
- describe the lifestyle of people in the community
- identify community events, celebrations, and pastimes

Activity Description:

As a class, discuss the special events and holiday celebrations observed by members of the local community. Invite students to share their own family traditions with others. Later, have learners describe their recreational activities. In a large group, conduct a survey of these popular pastimes and record the results on a graph.

Materials/Resources:
√ arts and crafts supplies
√ resource materials

```
┌─────────────────────────────────────────────┐
│              Medieval World                   │
│                                               │
│              Appetizers                       │
│         Boar's head with spices               │
│  Apples with grape sauce or orange sauce      │
│      Salad topped with delicious fruit        │
│     Vegetable Salad with sweet spices         │
│                                               │
│               Dinner                          │
│     Boiled salmon with Vegetable sauce        │
│        Stew with our finest cut fish          │
│         Beef with vegetable soup              │
│                                               │
│            Children's Meal                    │
│               Swan Soup                       │
│        Roasted Rabbit with nuts               │
│                                               │
│               Drinks                          │
│           Fine grape wine                     │
│             Apple juice                       │
│            Orange juice                       │
│             Fruit juice                       │
│                Milk                           │
└─────────────────────────────────────────────┘
```

Performance Tasks in Focus:
Developing a Want Ad, Making Community Goods and Providing Directions, Scheduling Life in the Community

Task Category:
developing writing skills—exploring text forms

Materials/Resources:
√ chart paper, markers

Ask students to research special events, celebrations, and recreational activities enjoyed by members of the community they are studying. They can locate information in literature collections, reference books, and other resource materials. Ask them to produce a list of pastimes, games, forms of entertainment, and festivities commemorated by these community groups. Have learners choose and do one of the following activities:

- Select a popular children's game from the time period you are studying, or one played by young people in the local community today. Research the origins of the game and find out how it is played. Invite others to participate in this game and explain how to play it.
- Design an invitation to a wedding or other special event taking place in the community you are studying. Be sure to include the date, time, special events, festivities, and list of gift ideas for this celebration.
- Produce a menu of foods served at a local restaurant, special celebration, or important event in the community.
- Plan a special event or celebration observed by members of the community you are studying, for example, a medieval feast or fair. Invite others to take part in this community festival.

Creating Texts About a Community

Specific Objectives for Students:
- identify and use the stages of the writing process
- produce writing using a variety of text forms or genres

Activity Description:

As a class, brainstorm and identify the stages of the writing process based on prior knowledge. Invite learners to share their personal writing experiences and products with others. Distribute copies of "The Steps in the Writing Process" which appears on the next page. Review important steps and procedures. Model the writing process for students by producing a short piece of writing related to the topic. Use the blackboard, chart paper, overheard projector or perhaps computer presentation software such as PowerPoint to display the text to students. Share effective writing strategies and techniques used during the various stages. Discuss the developments and changes noted in the text throughout each step of the process. Invite students to share their opinions of the final product.

The Steps in the Writing Process

1. Generate ideas through discussion and brainstorming.

2. Engage in pre-writing activities.
   a) *Choose a topic.*
   b) *Select a genre/format:*

narrative	report	classified ad
letter	procedure	magazine/newspaper article
journal	schedule	poem
non-fiction text	Other: _____	

   c) *Determine an audience:*

younger children	family members
adults	seniors
peers	Other: _____
students in other classes	

   d) *Establish a purpose:*

Entertain readers	Deliver instructions
Raise issues	Inform audiences
Outline/plan events	Record information
Provide explanations	Teach moral lessons
Persuade readers	Convey universal messages
Other: _____	

3. Prepare a writing plan. Options:

outline	web
diagram	story map
flowchart	story grammar
Other: _____	

4. Write a first draft.

5. Revise.

6. Produce a second draft.

7. Edit.

8. Proofread.

9. Create a final draft version.

10. Publish.

© 2003 *Authentic Assessment* by Katherine Luongo-Orlando. Pembroke Publishers. All rights reserved. Permission to reproduce for classroom use.

Provide learners with an opportunity to produce a piece of writing in a small or large group by using the steps in the writing process. First, have students imagine they are members of the community being studied. Ask them to reflect on previous lessons and summarize different aspects of community living—work, home, and recreation. As a class or in small groups, generate writing ideas through discussion and brainstorming. Together, select a topic, format, audience, and purpose for writing. Next, use chart paper, markers, or perhaps on overhead projector, to construct the text. After creating the rough copy, challenge students to revise their writing together and develop a second draft. They should then edit, proofread, and discuss changes as a group. To conclude, have students prepare a final draft version and publish the text they have been working on. Invite groups to share their products with others.

Understanding the Influence of Advertising

Mass media dominate so many aspects of society in the world today. Media products contain powerful messages that shape our values, beliefs, perceptions, and behaviors. Developing units of study around the media will enable students to understand and use them effectively. Focusing on the world of advertising, in particular, may inform young people of the media's persuasive influence. It will also provide opportunities for them to examine the creativity involved in the production of media works and to apply artistry and writing techniques to the construction of their own media products. Examining the nature of advertising may shape students into well-informed, insightful audiences and consumers who are critical of the media and not manipulated by them.

A focus on media literacy can provide students with authentic opportunities to develop critical thinking and communication skills they can apply to real life. The ability to use language persuasively to sell ideas, express opinions, and convince others to think a certain way is an important skill that children should develop. The instructional activities provided on the following pages have been developed around the media and the world of advertising. These learning experiences may provide young people with the critical understanding, voices, messages, and techniques they need to express ideas capable of influencing society as a whole.

Persuasive Writing in Everyday Life: An Introduction

Performance Tasks in Focus:
Developing a Product, Designing an Ad Layout, Packaging a Product, Creating Body Copy

Task Categories:
persuasive writing, media literacy

Materials/Resources:
√ bulletin board
√ art supplies
√ magazines, newspapers, telephone directories, promotional flyers

Specific Objectives for Students:
• locate examples of persuasive writing in the media
• identify a variety of media works
• describe the different forms of advertising in society

Activity Description:
Young people may be familiar with many forms of persuasive writing found in the media. As a class, take a walk throughout the school community and invite students to observe the different types of advertising, or persuasive writing, they see around them. Later, list these forms of advertising and brainstorm examples of other media works. Students may identify

• outdoor exhibits (bulletins, billboards, and posters)
• transit signs

- window displays
- newspaper and magazine ads
- television commercials
- radio promotions
- direct mail coupons and flyers
- telephone directories
- Internet Web site banners

Next, design a bulletin board or other visual display that illustrates the different types of advertising found in the environment. Encourage students to contribute items to the display board throughout the unit.

Examining Persuasive Media Works

Performance Tasks in Focus:
Developing a Product, Designing an Ad Layout, Packaging a Product, Creating Body Copy

Task Categories:
persuasive writing, media literacy

Materials/Resources:
√ newspaper and magazine ads
√ direct mail coupons and promotional flyers
√ posters
√ computer
√ VCR and videotape of television commercials
√ cassette player and audiotape of radio announcements
√ bulletin board
√ art supplies

Specific Objectives for Students:
- critically read, view and/or listen to different types of advertising
- identify the characteristics of media works
- understand the purpose of persuasive writing and explain how it is used to produce media works

Activity Description:

In small groups, have students examine the following forms of media:

- newspaper ads
- magazines ads
- direct mail coupons and promotional flyers
- posters and Internet Web site banners
- television commercials
- radio announcements

Ask learners to note the specific features of each type of advertisement and present their findings to others.

Discuss with the class what persuasive writing seeks to do. Students should understand that the intent may be to promote or sell ideas, to convince others, to persuade people to think or act in a particular way, or to influence or change people's actions or opinions.

Next, brainstorm ways that people try to achieve these objectives. Ideas should include use of powerful language, visual images, symbols, and media techniques, such as the use of slogans and professional endorsements.

As a class, identify the purpose of advertising and explain how the forms of media students observed are characteristic of persuasive writing. It is important for students to understand that the intent of advertising is to sell a product or service, or persuade people to think, feel, and act in a certain way. Use a graphic organizer, such as a flowchart, to record important concepts learned throughout the unit on the display board. Begin by featuring the words ADVERTISEMENTS SELL at the top of the flowchart. Next, examine the effective techniques used to promote products and make ads appealing.

Advertising Techniques

Performance Tasks in Focus:
Developing a Product, Designing
an Ad Layout, Packaging a
Product, Creating Body Copy

Task Categories:
media literacy, oral and visual
communication

Materials/Resources:
√ videotape of television
  commercials
√ audio-recording of radio ads
√ Internet Web site banner
  advertisements
√ print media, newspaper and
  magazine ads
√ bulletin board

Specific Objective for Students:
• identify the techniques used to produce different forms of media and advertising

Activity Description:

Select examples of a variety of media works to share with students. You might pre-pare a videotape of television commercials, an audio-recording of radio ads, and a sample of Web advertising banners, as well as choose ads from several print media, such as newspapers and magazines. As a class, produce a list of effective techniques used to make these advertisements appealing to others (e.g., color, music, dance, action, visual images, layout, print, sound/sound effects). Challenge learners to identify other methods that advertisers may use to promote or sell a product, for example,

- promotional offers and discounts
- testimonials by product users
- endorsements by famous people
- use of cartoon figures
- the pull of familiar experiences (e.g., a holiday tradition or daily event)

After examining media forms that use these specific sales techniques, encourage students to locate their own and classify them according to the advertising method used. Have learners include a list of effective sales techniques and appealing ad fea-tures on the flowchart and display samples on the media bulletin board.

Examining Print Media

Performance Tasks in Focus:
Designing an Ad Layout, Creating
Body Copy

Task Categories:
persuasive writing, media literacy

Materials/Resources:
√ examples of print media
  (newspaper and magazine ads,
  direct mail coupons,
  promotional flyers)

Specific Objectives for Students:
• identify text features in print media, including headlines and slogans
• describe the functions of each text feature and characteristics of print media

Activity Description:

Provide examples of persuasive writing from various print media sources, includ-ing newspaper and magazine ads, direct mail coupons, and promotional flyers. As a class, identify the characteristics of these forms of advertisement. For example:

- a headline, with main message or introduction
- a slogan, or a catchy phrase to attract attention
- a product description, including uses and features
- testimonials, or statements of opinion, by product users
- endorsements by famous people/testimonials by celebrity users
- a product character—fictional/cartoon character who delivers the sales mes-sage
- product comparisons, where leading products are compared to competitive brands and advantages are given

Invite students to locate their own samples of print media from various sources. Using the ads they have collected, have learners work with others to label each characteristic and determine the meaning or function of the features noted above. Challenge students to produce concise definitions for each term and to provide explanations and real examples. To consolidate their understanding of these char-acteristics of print advertisements, invite learners to share their findings with others and reach a consensus on the meaning of each feature listed above. For future reference, students may post the samples of print media that they have labelled on the media display board.

Design Features of Print Media

Performance Tasks in Focus:
Designing an Ad Layout, Creating Body Copy

Task Categories:
persuasive writing, media literacy, visual communication

Materials/Resources:
√ a variety of electronic media, television, and radio ads
√ print media

Specific Objectives for Students:

- identify basic features and design elements in print media, including logo, type-face, and layout
- describe the standard format of ad layouts

Activity Description:

As a class, compare and contrast the presentation features and advertising techniques used in a variety of media works—television commercials, radio promotions, electronic media and print ads. Next, examine the specific design elements found in newspaper and magazine advertisements and list general characteristics. Your list will probably include

- visual images, such as photos or illustrations of product
- graphics, for example, a logo
- color
- typeface (font and size of print)
- size of ad
- layout, or arrangement of elements
- page format

Ask students to compare and contrast these design features in print ads they have collected.

Select ads with common layout features and formats that include a headline, slogan, product description, visual image, graphic logo, brand name label, and other standard parts. For each newspaper and magazine advertisement chosen, cut apart the layout features and place the sections in an envelope. Each envelope should include the parts of only one newspaper or magazine advertisement. Next, divide students into cooperative groups. Provide each group with an envelope. Challenge the students in each group to reassemble the ad, noting particular design features, including size of ad and typeface, as they work. Let groups reconstruct a variety of newspaper and magazine advertisements in order to consolidate their understanding of the characteristics and design elements of print media. As a class, review the standard formats of ad layouts.

Ad Word Bank

Performance Tasks in Focus:
Packaging a Product, Creating Body Copy

Task Categories:
vocabulary development, persuasive writing

Specific Objectives for Students:

- select effective vocabulary from a variety of media works
- understand specific terminology used to describe media products
- produce a list of vocabulary words that can be used for persuasive writing

Activity Description:

Read a variety of newspaper and magazine advertisements to the class, and have students read several print ads independently. As a large group, compare and contrast the writing styles used in these media works. Discuss the similarities and differences between print media and other forms of writing (e.g., narrative, letter,

Materials/Resources:
√ newspaper and magazine ads
√ strips of paper
√ chart paper

essay, and report). Since advertisements provide an effective example of persuasive writing, review the features of this form of writing noted in the media works.

Next, examine the use of effective word choices, compact phrasing, detailed expressions, and concise product descriptions found in print ads. Have students locate examples of short, catchy phrases, sentence fragments, puns and invented spelling used in newspaper and magazine advertisements. Later, discuss the reasons why advertisers use compressed language, catchy slogans, incomplete sentences and limited text in ads published in newspapers and magazines (mainly to reduce print costs and build audience appeal).

Ask students to work in partners or small groups. Have them select catchy phrases, slogans, descriptive words, and other language forms from the print ads they have collected and record them on strips of paper. Invite students to share examples they located with the whole class. As a large group, arrange the strips to form a vocabulary list on chart paper, a bulletin board, or other visual display. Encourage students to use the ad word bank throughout the unit.

Advertising Appeal

Performance Tasks in Focus:
Developing a Product, Creating Body Copy

Task Categories:
persuasive writing, media literacy, visual communication

Materials/Resources:
√ a variety of media works

Specific Objectives for Students:
• identify the persuasive techniques used by advertisers to make a product or service appealing to potential buyers or consumers
• classify a variety of advertisements according to basic forms of appeal—factual, emotional, and sensory

Activity Description:

Invite students to identify attractive features of advertisements they have encountered and discuss the effectiveness of these ads with others. Read a variety of newspaper and magazine advertisements to the class. Share examples of other media works, such as television commercials and radio ads. Discuss the ways in which advertisers try to make the product or service seem appealing to consumers. Introduce students to the following types of appeal: factual, emotional, and sensory.

Begin by examining the persuasive message in a variety of print ads. To do this, provide samples of media works that include basic facts, characteristics, and features of a product/service, and have students identify the type of information presented in the ad. Explain to students that advertisements that provide specific details or actual reports on a consumer product or service use factual appeal to attract informed buyers. Here, the ad message is presented in a *factual* way to persuade consumers.

Next, share examples of advertisements that describe how a particular product makes a user or client feel. Explain to students that ads that suggest a consumer item or service will provide personal satisfaction and improve lifestyle rely on *emotional* appeal to attract consumers. Ads that use this approach might appeal to a person's need for happiness, love, fame, and security by suggesting ways the product or service will satisfy that need.

Then, examine media works that arouse the senses, for example, food ads. Begin with visual images in print ads and television commercials and have students describe their reaction to the presentation of food in these media works. Explain to students that when advertisers attempt to make a food item attractive, they are using *appetite* appeal to lure buyers.

If you are using those old laundry detergents that are not making your kid's clothes clean now you have a chance to get your family's clothes fresh. Fire tide has fast-acting cleaning power that fights stains and leaves laundry smelling fresh and looking clean. If you're not pleased with our laundry detergent, you'll get your money back.

Product description

Performance Task in Focus:
Developing a Product

Task Categories:
organizing information, analyzing and synthesizing information, persuasive writing

Materials/Resources:
√ a variety of print advertisements
√ "Commercial Log" handout

COMMERCIAL LOG

DIRECTIONS TO STUDENTS.
Keep a log of the type of commercials featured on television at different times of the day (e.g. morning, afternoon, dinner hour, evening). Record the types of commercials that appear on different channels or network stations (e.g. sports network, news/weather channel, children's network, family channel, local stations). Prepare to share your findings with others.

Time of Day	Type of Commercial (Featured Product)	Channel/ Network Station
Morning	cereal	Channel/8
Morning	chocolate	channel/6
morning	cars	channel/4
after noon	Bags	channel/89
after noon	Shoes	channel/87
after noon	dresses	channel/85
after noon	Lunch bags	channel/63
afternoon	Soaps	channel/25

To reaffirm their understanding of this sales tactic, present students with advertisements for several cleaning products. As a group, select effective word choices and vivid expressions used to describe the items presented in the ads (e.g., "fast-acting cleaning power," "gentle fresh smell," "removes tough stains and ground-in dirt"). By using descriptive phrases and powerful visual images, advertisers, here, use *sensory* appeal to attract consumers and persuade them to purchase the product.

After introducing students to these basic forms of appeal, ask them to locate specific examples of media works that rely on each of these marketing techniques. Challenge learners to classify advertisements according to those that use *factual, emotional,* or *sensory* (e.g., appetite) appeal to attract buyers. Conclude with a discussion of the type of appeal that they personally find most effective.

Raising Audience Awareness

Specific Objectives for Students:
• view and analyze patterns in commercial broadcasting
• identify audiences commonly targeted by the media
• specify consumer products aimed at selected groups

Activity Description:
Invite students to keep a log of the type of commercials featured on television at different times of the day from various channels or network stations available to them. Students with limited access to TV stations can do a comparison of the ads found on two different networks or local community channels. Students without access to a television can complete the activity with a peer. Alternatively, teachers can videotape a series of commercials from various stations and have students view them at school. Have learners record their findings on a copy of the "Commercial Log" provided on page 75. As a class, discuss the results of their research. Challenge them to classify the types of advertisements featured on television throughout the day (e.g., food, cleaning/home improvement, personal care, toy, and car). Have learners identify the different groups these commercials are aimed at. Discuss the reasons why certain advertisements are featured at a particular time of day. For example, toy ads often appear before and after school on television channels that air popular children's programs. The intent is to attract children as consumers. Ask students to identify other consumer products advertised on television that are aimed at specific audiences.

As a class, make a list of target audiences, or different groups of consumers that products are aimed at. These may include children, teens, young adults, parents, women, men, and seniors.

Collect a variety of print ads from different newspapers and types of magazines (e.g., business, fashion, home, parent, and sport). Have students work together to identify the target audience of each ad and to arrange the ads into categories. Ask learners to review the ads they have classified and produce a list of consumer products aimed at each group. The items below are often targeted at the following consumer groups:

Try the best low fat cake ever!

Sweet'n low is the best cake mix ever! It's low in fat with a delicious and a fruity taste. The sparkles come in five different flavours: orange, grape, apple, banana and strawberry. Everyone will love it!

It's so light, it's going to rise.

Print ad

Performance Task in Focus:
Developing a Product

Task Categories:
gathering information, process learning, persuasive writing

Materials/Resources:
√ chart or graph paper
√ children's toys, games, and electronics
√ samples of new food products

Children	Teens
toys	electronics
cereal	cell phones
cookies	snack foods
luncheon foods	personal care products (e.g., makeup)

Invite students to display print ads featuring a range of products aimed at different consumer groups on the media board. Once learners are aware of target audiences and can identify the types of consumer goods aimed at different groups, they are ready to learn about how products are developed.

Product Development

Specific Objectives for Students:

• participate in surveys, product tests, and consumer sampling experiences
• understand the role of consumers in the development of a new product
• identify and use the steps in the product development process

Activity Description:

Conduct a class survey of children's favorite breakfast foods and record the results on a graph. Use the results of the survey to determine the type of breakfast food most popular among the group surveyed.

Later, bring in or ask students to bring in a variety of children's toys, games, and electronics. Distribute these to students working in groups, and ask them to test each product. Invite learners to share their opinion of each product tested.

Arrange a visit to a local supermarket, or prepare samples of a variety of new food products for students to taste. Ask children to comment on the items they have sampled.

As a class, discuss how consumer surveys, product testing, and sampling can be effectively used to develop a new product. Brainstorm a list of steps that are part of the product development process. For example:

1. Involve consumers. Conduct surveys, test the product, offer samples.
2. Create a name for the product.
3. Outline the product's uses.
4. Describe important features.
5. Explain the *point of difference*, what makes the product better than other similar items on the market.

Invite students to imagine that they are members of an advertising and marketing firm. Have them work in small groups. Challenge them to follow the process outlined above to develop a new product:

• a food item
• a cleaning material (e.g., laundry detergent, broom, or spray bottle)
• a skin and health care product (e.g., soap bars or shampoo)
• other household good
• an office or school supply
• a toy or game

Later, hold a "production meeting" where groups can present their ideas to others.

Commercial Log

DIRECTIONS TO STUDENTS:

Keep a log of the types of commercials featured on television at different times of the day. Record the types of commercials that appear on different channels or network stations, for example, sports network, news/weather channel, children's network, family channel, and local stations. Prepare to share your findings with others.

Time of Day	Type of Commercial (Featured Product)	Channel/Network Station

© 2003 *Authentic Assessment* by Katherine Luongo-Orlando. Pembroke Publishers. All rights reserved. Permission to reproduce for classroom use.

Conducting Market Research

Performance Task in Focus:
Developing a Product

Task Categories:
gathering information, analyzing and synthesizing information, vocabulary development

Materials/Resources:
√ various brands of consumer products

Specific Objectives for Students:

• conduct market research on consumer products
• understand and use specific terminology to describe consumer goods

Activity Description:

Conducting competitive research on consumer goods is an important part of product development. To do this in the classroom, divide the students into groups and ask each group to select a product that they want to investigate. To begin their market research, groups should first identify all the competitive brands of the same consumer good. After locating the different brands of such a product as laundry detergent, challenge students to identify the *point of difference.* In other words, they should note the features that set each brand apart (e.g., lemon fresh smell, whitening agents, cleaning power).

Throughout their research, students may discover that some consumer products, perhaps toothpaste, have common features and little, if any, point of difference. Instead, learners may encounter a *difference in branding.* Here, the brand name label and product packaging are especially designed to attract a certain audience and create a need for the consumer good among members of this target group. For example, a company may develop a new brand of laundry detergent with the same effective ingredients as other detergents, but market the product using a chic package design and trendy label to attract a younger or stylish group of consumers.

Following their market research, invite groups to share their findings with the class. Compare and contrast the results of these investigations. Summarize the importance of this step in product development.

Product Description

Performance Task in Focus:
Creating Body Copy

Task Category:
persuasive writing

Materials/Resources:
√ consumer packages
√ magazine and newspaper ads

Specific Objectives for Students:

• identify the text features of product descriptions
• use vocabulary effectively to describe a product
• begin to write persuasively to convince others

Activity Description:

Read the product description of different consumer goods advertised in magazines or newspapers to the class. Have students examine the text on consumer packages and other print media. Compare and contrast this format with other types of writing.

As a large group, produce a list of features included in product descriptions. The content may include

• summary of the product
• purpose/use
• any research findings or statistics
• distinguishing features that set a product apart from other competing brands, that is, the point of difference

Using the information they learned from their market research, have students work with others to write a product description for a consumer good that has just been improved or upgraded. Encourage students to use vocabulary from the ad

The Super Deluxe Computer lets your worries go. It is virus free and has a DVD player. It is voice activated. Just say "Do my homework"! It will do it. Comes with a hand massager and a big screen. Make your own movies if you like. Now available in a pack of three only for $1000.

76

word bank and persuasive language to write their product descriptions. Invite students to share the media works they have created and offer feedback to others. Display samples on the media bulletin board.

Slogans

Performance Tasks in Focus:
Designing an Ad Layout, Creating Body Copy

Task Categories:
persuasive writing, oral communication

Materials/Resources:
√ print advertisements
√ bulletin board
√ strips of paper

Specific Objectives for Students:

- describe important text features of print media, notably slogans
- identify slogans in various print advertisements
- understand the messages conveyed in slogans
- make product associations between consumer goods and slogans

Activity Description:

In the world of advertising, companies often use slogans to draw attention to a product. A slogan is usually a short, catchy phrase that is easy to remember. During an ad campaign, the slogan is used repeatedly to attract buyers and develop product association. This motto, or expression, is designed to help create a favorable image of both the company and the consumer good.

Prompt learners to share examples of slogans they remember. Next, ask them to identify slogans from the newspaper and magazine ads they collected previously. As a class, examine the placement of the slogan on the ad layout. Have students cut out slogans from print media and post them on a display board or chart. In groups, invite learners to practise saying slogans using a variety of drama and read-aloud techniques, such as choral speaking, expressive voice, and special effects. Later, have students create different matching games that challenge others to identify popular slogans and the company or product that uses them. Finally, have learners play the various matching games that they created.

Testimonials

Performance Task in Focus:
Creating Body Copy

Task Category:
persuasive writing

Materials/Resources:
√ media works featuring testimonials

Specific Objectives for Students:

- select and understand the use of product endorsements
- describe the persuasive influence of testimonials in the promotion of consumer goods
- plan and conduct a consumer survey, product test, or sampling of an item
- use persuasive language to convince others

Activity Description:

Advertisements that feature endorsements contain testimonials. A *testimonial* is a statement made by a product user describing his or her reaction, feelings, and opinion about a consumer good/service. These endorsements can be used to persuade people to purchase a product and create customer loyalty.

Share with the class examples of a variety of persuasive media works that contain testimonials and ask students to select their own. As a large group, list the types of people that appear in product endorsements. Examples include

- an average user or ordinary consumer
- a movie/TV star
- a popular athlete
- a music group or singer
- a person famous for other reasons

"Super Crunchy Cereal makes me stronger everyday."

Performance Tasks in Focus:
Designing an Ad Layout, Packaging a Product, Creating Body Copy

Task Category:
persuasive writing

Materials/Resources:
√ consumer packages
√ print advertisements

Super Mini Chocolate Gummy Cookies.
This marvelous cookie is sweet and delicious. It has no fat. This tasty cookie is filled with different chocolate flavours. You'll love the low price and the good taste.

"Super Mini Chocolate Gummy Cookies is the most delicious cookie ever made."

Performance Task in Focus:
Packaging a Product

Task Categories:
following instructions, procedural writing

Materials/Resources:
√ consumer packages
√ consumer product (e.g., microwave popcorn)
√ chart paper

Have students identify current products being advertised by famous people and discuss the effectiveness of using celebrity endorsements to promote consumer goods. If the product being advertised by the celebrity suits his or her public image, the endorsement can be a persuasive way of influencing the public to buy the product. Consumers may trust the celebrity's word.

In groups, have students plan and conduct a survey, product test, or sampling of an item on the market. Encourage learners to participate in these consumer events. After students have sampled or used a variety of consumer goods, ask them to interview each other about the products and record testimonials given by different users. Have learners share the testimonials they have written and post examples on the media board.

Becoming Copywriters

Specific Objectives for Students:
- examine, read, and discuss the text features of product packages and ad layouts
- identify basic elements of body copy, in other words, product description, slogan, testimonials, and other details
- use persuasive writing to produce body copy for existing consumer products

Activity Description:

Display a variety of product packages and print advertisements to the class. Have students examine the writing featured on the package design and ad layout. This text is often referred to as the *body copy*. As a class, produce a list of print items included in the body copy, such as a product description, a slogan, testimonials, promotional offers, such as a contest with entry forms, and any additional writing that appears on the ad (e.g., contact information).

Have learners imagine they are copywriters who have just been hired by an advertising agency to write the text that will appear on the product package and ad layout. Ask students to work with others to develop the body copy for existing products or for consumer goods created in previous activities. Remind them to use persuasive writing and vocabulary from the ad word bank in their body copy. As part of the writing process, learners should be encouraged to brainstorm ideas, produce a rough draft, edit and revise their writing with others, and publish the final copy that will appear in print on the package design or ad layout.

Procedural Writing

Specific Objectives for Students:
- identify the text features of procedural writing
- record and follow instructions for making consumer goods

Activity Description:

Collect a variety of consumer packages that feature instructions on the box. In groups, have students read the instructions provided on each product package displayed in the collection. As a class, identify features of procedural writing used on the consumer products. Instructions on packages usually provide a clear and concise step-by-step explanation of how to use the product.

Next, display a box of microwave popcorn or another popular consumer product. With the class, brainstorm a list of steps that explain how to prepare this item. Using clear and concise language, record the steps in sequence on chart paper or

Instructions:
1. Take the fries out of the freezer.
2. Cut the bag open and put the fries on a baking tray.
3. Turn the oven on to 400F.
4. Put the fries in the oven.
5. Leave them in oven for 5 minutes.
6. Open the oven and take the tray out.
7. Pour the fries into a bowel (or in a plate).
8. Add ketchup, vinegar, butter, salt or other topping.

MacMan Frozen Fries

Performance Tasks in Focus:
Developing a Product, Designing an Ad Layout, Packaging a Product, Creating Body Copy

Task Categories:
visual communication, media literacy

Materials/Resources:
√ consumer packages
√ measuring tapes, scales, etc.
√ construction materials for packages

the chalkboard. Finally, invite volunteers to follow the instructions the class has written by either making the actual product or developing a role-play scenario. By having volunteers carry out the procedures students have developed, the class can ensure that the instructions are presented in the proper sequence and that all important steps are included. Provide additional opportunities for students to practise procedural writing and following instructions, if needed.

Product Packaging

Specific Objectives for Students:
• identify the text features, visuals, and design elements on product packages
• use mathematical concepts and skills to investigate product packages
• construct a variety of product packages

Activity Description:
Arrange a trip to a supermarket, or encourage students to visit one with their family or friends. Ask them to examine consumer products while shopping, noting packaging designs, sizes, and prices. Invite students to bring in from home a variety of cartons, boxes, and other packages for consumer goods and create a display of their items in the classroom. In groups, have them examine the information on product packages and compare important features. These include

- brand names and flavors
- photos and illustrations
- logos and graphics
- colors
- package materials (e.g., metal or plastic)
- quantity of goods (mass or capacity)
- units of measurement
- product description
- promotional offers and coupons
- other related items (e.g., nutritional information and instructions)

Provide opportunities for learners to explore the features of product packages in a variety of ways. Encourage students to sort packages according to different attributes, such as shape, size, color, price, information on labels, content of packages, and mass or capacity. Challenge students to take measurements of a variety of product packages. For example, they can use rulers to measure length, width, height, perimeter, and area.

Next, examine the various ways in which consumer packages are constructed. Provide students with empty cardboard packages to unfold. Then, display the unfolded packages, identify the shapes of each container (e.g., rectangular prism, cube, or triangular prism) and compare the *nets*, or outlines of unfolded product packages. Have learners reassemble the unfolded cardboard packages. Challenge students to construct a variety of solid containers to prepare them for the design of their own consumer packages. Learners can practise creating their own product packages by

- opening up empty boxes, placing them flat on a sheet of paper, tracing the pattern of unfolded packages, cutting out the nets, folding the edges, and using the tabs to assemble the nets into solids again

- unfolding packages, tracing the faces, cutting apart the faces, and then taping the faces together to form consumer packages
- using blackline masters of nets available in math resource books to make geometric solids (e.g., nets for a triangular pyramid or square pyramid)

Once young people have had an opportunity to construct product packages, they can begin to examine the visuals and graphic design features of these consumer goods.

Graphic Design

Performance Tasks in Focus:
Designing an Ad Layout,
Packaging a Product

Task Categories:
visual communication, media literacy

Materials/Resources:
√ consumer packages
√ art supplies
√ computer software, especially multimedia software and graphic design programs

Specific Objectives for Students:
- examine the graphic design elements on consumer packages
- describe the work of professionals involved in designing product packages
- redesign logos, visuals, graphic designs, and symbols featured on consumer packages using a variety of materials

Activity Description:
As a class, examine the designs on product packages and labels found on a variety of consumer goods. Have students note such features as print/lettering, artwork, graphics, colors, lines, and shapes.

Explain that artists design the packages and labels that students see on consumer products. The artists who create the designs on product packages are called *graphic designers*. They plan the artwork, labels, lettering, and other visuals to attract buyers and persuade consumers to purchase goods and services.

In groups, have students select a consumer product they want to investigate, perhaps cereal or toothpaste. Challenge each group to locate some product packages for the consumer good they selected and create a display, for example, all brand name packages of laundry detergent. Next, have groups study the design on brand name labels and packages, focusing on distinguishing features. They will probably note

- style of lettering (Brand name labels on laundry detergents are often large and block-like.)
- colors (Most laundry detergent boxes are bright and intense in color.)
- shapes (Laundry detergent boxes often have swirling shapes.)
- symbols (Laundry detergent boxes often use target-like designs.)
- other visual elements

Later, invite each group to present their findings to the class, noting specific design features that appear on brand name packages of popular consumer goods. Discuss the functions of an effective package design.

Have students imagine they are graphic designers for an advertising company. Provide learners with a variety of art materials and resources, including computer software programs. Challenge students to redesign or recreate the labels and product packages for existing consumer products by using an art medium of their choice. Display the artwork they produce on the media board.

Presenting to an Audience

Performance Tasks in Focus:
Developing a Product, Designing an Ad Layout, Creating Body Copy, Packaging a Product

Task Categories:
oral language, visual communication

Materials/Resources:
√ audio-visual equipment
√ art supplies
√ computer software, especially multimedia software and graphic design programs

Specific Objectives for Students:
- improve oral and visual communication skills
- develop presentation tools and methods of communicating information to an audience

Activity Description:

Invite students to select a media project already completed in this unit. Provide learners with a variety of presentation tools, audio-visual equipment, and other supplies that can be used to display their media works to others. Encourage students to demonstrate their learning in several ways. Learners can design a visual presentation to showcase their final products, such as a newspaper or magazine edition, a consumer display, or an exhibition, such as a trade fair or advertising convention. Students can plan oral presentations to demonstrate their media works to others, such as an ad campaign, a product launch, or a production meeting. Young people can be challenged to use other types of technology, for example, electronic equipment, to produce radio advertisements, television commercials, or other media formats to present their work to others.

Once students have selected a communication method they are comfortable with, ask them to study and identify effective criteria and features of the presentation tool they have chosen. They might examine various consumer displays, listen to several radio announcements, or view a variety of television commercials, for example. Allow learners to adequately plan and produce an oral or visual presentation that incorporates the characteristics of the selected format. Finally, encourage students to communicate their work with others and provide feedback to peers.

Aligning Instructional Activities with the Performance Task

A unit of study, developed around literature, community, the media, or another relevant topic, may require several weeks to a month in instruction time to adequately prepare students for the performance task. Throughout the unit, provide learning experiences that will enable students to build conceptual knowledge, practise important skills, and develop essential work habits required for the assessment. In the meantime, provide support to children with special needs, gather evidence of students' learning, collect work samples for portfolios, and address curriculum expectations in other program areas.

Following the unit, allow learners to share products created during the lessons, such as picture dictionaries, drama presentations, responses to literature and artwork. Prior to the assessment, summarize important concepts, strategies, and attitudes introduced in the instructional activities that are closely aligned with the performance task. The connection between learning experiences in the unit and the assessment can be made by reviewing key features, vocabulary, information, routines, thinking skills, procedures, models, and presentation tools that students can use to do the task. Understanding the learning context may enable young people to realize how relevant instructional activities can be in the real-life application of knowledge, skills, and work habits in authentic assessment situations. Once this connection is made, and students are adequately prepared and motivated, begin the assessment period by administering the performance task.

Administering the Assessment

In the past, assessment and evaluation of student learning was defined largely by test results, unit projects, or other summative methods. Administration procedures for these tasks required instructions in test taking, research, report writing, and other essential skills. The move towards authentic assessment practices has introduced new implementation methods designed to improve student achievement. As teachers develop performance tasks that are embedded into the curriculum, young people are able to demonstrate their learning through meaningful, engaging, and inspiring experiences that reflect classroom activities. In performance-based programs, preparations for the assessment become part of the instructional strategies. Prior to implementation, students have an opportunity to acquire the prerequisite knowledge, skills, and work habits needed for the assessment.

The guidelines provided below will assist you with the administration of performance-based assessment tasks.

Parameter Setting for Performance

As part of the implementation process, inform students of the focus goal and outline the learning expectations that will be addressed by the performance task. Understanding the objectives will guide students through the assessment and improve results. As part of the administration process, post the focus goal and curriculum expectations in the classroom to ensure that all participants understand them and use them as reference tools to assess their performance.

Next, introduce the performance task. Provide students with directions to lead them through the assessment. (See the set of student instructions designed to assist learners with the performance tasks developed in this book. They appear on pages 84 to 97.)

Specify the performance criteria and standards for judging students' work. Share assessment and evaluation tools that have been developed, or devise scoring procedures with students. Examine work samples to determine the features of quality work, levels of achievement, and standards of excellence. Indicate the content knowledge, process skills, and attitudes that will be assessed.

Schedule time for the assessment. The complex nature of the performance task may require students to work over an extended period. Integrated learning experiences may entail changes to programs, schedules, and timetables in order to provide students with the blocks of time needed to complete the task. Be flexible with programming during the assessment period. After a unit of study, which may require up to one month in instruction time and preparation, the assessment period may last anywhere from one to two weeks depending on the complexity of the task and the specific performance requirements.

Prior to implementation, gather the support materials, equipment, and resources that will assist students during the assessment. Arrange the learning environment to allow students space to complete the performance task. Designate areas in the classroom where assessment materials, required resources, equipment, and students' ongoing work can be stored. Display boards, shelves, assessment folders, work stations, and learning centres would prove useful.

Provide students with general strategies and tools that will improve their overall performance. In order to meet the needs of individual children, such as those with special needs or learning English as a second language, program modifications may need to be made. These modifications may include reducing the task requirements, providing more resources (e.g., picture dictionaries), allocating more time, and allowing students to work with a resource teacher or volunteer.

Review potential audiences and formats for students' work. If possible, allow students to select their own audience, perhaps peers, younger students, or parents, and determine a presentation format (see page 11). Display samples, models, or exemplars that illustrate different levels of performance and formats for students' work.

The Performance Task as Classwork

Before administering the performance task, inform parents and students of the upcoming assessment period and review important guidelines. Unlike homework assignments and projects, performance assessments must be completed at school. Students can thereby demonstrate their knowledge, skills, and work habits independently. Allow students to work collaboratively with others and to use available resources and support materials to complete the task. However, final products must be completed individually unless the assessment instructions indicate that the performance task should be done in pairs or cooperative groups. Parents can support learners during the assessment period by discussing their child's progress on the performance task, helping them locate additional resources, equipment, and materials that can be brought to school, and providing learning strategies and encouragement that will help students succeed.

The above guidelines for implementation may be supported by other effective strategies. In addition to assisting learners, these implementation procedures ensure that teachers have time to monitor students throughout the assessment. Once the performance task has been administered, teachers can begin the process of gathering evidence of student progress.

The performance task instructions and worksheets on pages 84 to 97 can be adapted or modified to meet students' needs and to support assessment planning for a variety of grade levels.

Writing a Sequel

Imagine that you are the author of a picture book, novel, short story, or other work of fiction you have recently read. Plan and write a sequel to the story, perhaps an additional chapter. In order to ensure that your story is a logical continuation of the original text, make sensible predictions and remember to include the following:

- the same basic elements of story (characters, theme, plot, and setting)
- accurate character portrayals
- reasonable changes to selected aspects of the narrative
- logical additions to the story (e.g., new characters and settings)
- related story conflicts and resolutions
- natural and correct use of dialogue throughout the story
- effective style of writing, literary devices, and language that flows well with the existing story
- information to ensure that there are no unexplained "gaps" between the original story and the sequel

Once you have considered these important components, create a story outline in which you brainstorm ideas for your setting, characters, plot, conflict, resolution, and theme.

Now, write a rough draft of your sequel. Be sure to include detailed descriptions and elements of distinctive writing.

Then, share your story with a peer in a writing conference.

Later, edit and revise your sequel.

Finally, publish your story.

© 2003 *Authentic Assessment* by Katherine Luongo-Orlando. Pembroke Publishers. All rights reserved. Permission to reproduce for classroom use.

Oral Retelling

Select a picture book, novel, short story, or other work of literature you are interested in reading, but have not read or heard before. Read the text independently. If you have selected a novel, read the opening chapter or a subsequent chapter only.

Prepare to share your chosen narrative with others by retelling it orally. Plan and practise your oral retelling by

- rereading the story to yourself
- reading selected parts of the story aloud to others
- identifying the basic elements of story
- noting the sequence of events
- creating a story map
- using storytelling aids and props
- producing a written recount of the story
- recording the oral retelling on cassette tape
- exploring oral language techniques, for example, changing pace, voice, pitch, and volume
- using selected words and phrases from the original story

Now that you have practised your oral recount, imagine that you are going to tell the story to a friend or peer who has not read or heard the story before.

Prepare a five minute summary to share. Then, tell the story to your teacher as naturally and confidently as you would share it with others.

© 2003 *Authentic Assessment* by Katherine Luongo-Orlando. Pembroke Publishers. All rights reserved. Permission to reproduce for classroom use.

Making a Community or Historical Map

Imagine that you are a cartographer, or map-maker, hired to produce a map of a community. The community may be in either the past or the present.

1. Select an area or topic for your map related to the unit you are studying. Possible topics might include
   - a local landmark
   - a pioneer village
   - a medieval manor/estate
   - an early settlement of immigrants
   - an Aboriginal community
   - an ancient civilization (Mediterranean, African, Asian, Central/South American)
   - an explorer's trade route

2. Research and make a list of important features (e.g., places, landmarks, buildings, and natural resources) found in the community you selected.

3. Develop symbols to represent the various landmarks, features, and places you identified above.

4. Produce a sketch map of the area you selected. Be sure to include the distinguishing features identified previously.

5. Reproduce the map in detail. Remember to consider the following components in the final phases of map construction:
   - title
   - labels
   - color
   - cardinal directions
   - legend
   - scale

© 2003 *Authentic Assessment* by Katherine Luongo-Orlando. Pembroke Publishers. All rights reserved. Permission to reproduce for classroom use.

Developing a Want Ad

Imagine that you are a writer for a community newspaper in charge of developing want ads for the Classified section.

1. Review the types of occupations held by members of the community you are studying.

2. Select an occupation you are interested in learning more about.

3. Use a variety of resource materials to research fully the occupation you selected.

4. Make a list of skills, education, experience, and other requirements necessary for the job.

5. Examine the classified ads in local newspapers, noting important features.

6. Produce a want ad or job posting for the occupation you selected.
   Be sure to consider the following items while writing your ad:
   - job description
   - qualifications required
   - application process
   - payment and benefits

7. Revise and edit the job posting you have written.

8. Publish the want ad that will appear in the Classified section of the newspaper.

© 2003 *Authentic Assessment* by Katherine Luongo-Orlando. Pembroke Publishers. All rights reserved. Permission to reproduce for classroom use.

Developing a Want Ad

TOPIC/UNIT/TIME PERIOD: _____

Type of Occupation: _____
_____

Job Description (summary, duties, responsibilities): _____
_____
_____
_____
_____

Qualifications (skills, education, experience required): _____
_____
_____
_____
_____

Application Process: _____
_____
_____
_____
_____
_____

Payment and Benefits: _____
_____
_____
_____
_____
_____

WANT AD
_____
_____
_____
_____
_____
_____
_____
_____
_____

© 2003 *Authentic Assessment* by Katherine Luongo-Orlando. Pembroke Publishers. All rights reserved. Permission to reproduce for classroom use.

Scheduling Life in the Community

Imagine that you are an active member of the community you are studying.

List important aspects of your everyday life. These will include
- daily chores, duties, and responsibilities
- type of job or work you are involved in
- community events that you like to participate in
- important celebrations and festivities that you like to attend
- pastimes and recreational activities that you enjoy

Now, arrange these items on a schedule that specifies the tasks, activities, and events that are part of your life in the community.

Be sure to consider the following elements when producing your schedule:
- time allotments/periods
- list of activities
- task descriptions
- sequence of events
- arrangement/layout, for example, chart, list, or table

Remember to use the steps in the writing process to develop the schedule outlined above.

© 2003 *Authentic Assessment* by Katherine Luongo-Orlando. Pembroke Publishers. All rights reserved. Permission to reproduce for classroom use.

Making Community Goods and Providing Directions

Imagine that you are a member of the community you are studying.

Review the list of cultural artifacts, food items, craft objects, or community goods developed previously. Select an item or activity you are interested in. You might choose

- a recipe
- a toy or game
- a household item (e.g., soap or candles)
- a daily chore (e.g., preserving food)
- a handmade good (e.g., a quilt, tapestry, or pottery)
- a home remedy (e.g., cough or cold medicine)

Gather the required materials and equipment. Use the information you located in your research to reproduce the object.

Please note: Some projects may require adult supervision. Consult a teacher, parent, or adult volunteer for guidance.

Devise a set of instructions that will assist others in making the same item you produced. Be sure that your directions describe the procedures fully and clearly.

Remember to include the following features:

- title
- headings (e.g., ingredients, method)
- connecting words: *first, then, after, when, once,* etc.
- factual details, information, and descriptions, including type and quantity of materials, time requirements, and precise measurements
- step-by-step guidelines/instructions
- diagrams, photographs, or labelled drawings

Be sure to use the steps in the writing process to develop your procedures.

© 2003 *Authentic Assessment* by Katherine Luongo-Orlando. Pembroke Publishers. All rights reserved. Permission to reproduce for classroom use.

Task Instructions for Students

Developing a Product

Develop a product that you want to sell.

1. To select a consumer good, plan and conduct market research, surveys, product testing, or sampling to determine what buyers need. Find out consumers' response to existing products related to the one you want to develop.

2. Select a target audience for your product.

3. Brainstorm possible names for your consumer good.

4. Determine the purpose and uses for your product.

5. Highlight important features of this consumer good. Describe what makes this product better than other similar items on the market (*point of difference*).

6. Select a sales technique that you will use to promote your product. Options include testimonials by ordinary users, endorsements by famous people, and product comparisons.

7. Choose a type of appeal that will attract buyers (factual, emotional, or sensory). Consider how you will use this appeal to advertise your product.

8. Record your ideas on the "Developing a Product" student worksheet.

9. Share your ideas with others in a "production meeting"—class discussion, small-group session, teacher/student conference, or peer conference.

© 2003 *Authentic Assessment* by Katherine Luongo-Orlando. Pembroke Publishers. All rights reserved. Permission to reproduce for classroom use.

Developing a Product

Type of Product: _____
_____
_____

Plan for Market Research, Survey, Product Test, or Sampling
(steps, questions, materials, etc.):

_____
_____
_____
_____
_____
_____
_____
_____
_____

Results of Market Research, Survey, Product Test, or Sampling:_____
_____
_____
_____
_____
_____

Target Audience: _____
_____

Name of Product: _____
_____

Purpose/Uses: _____
_____

Point of Difference (distinguishing features): _____
_____

Sales Technique: _____
_____

Type of Appeal: _____
_____
_____

© 2003 *Authentic Assessment* by Katherine Luongo-Orlando. Pembroke Publishers. All rights reserved. Permission to reproduce for classroom use.

Creating Body Copy

Imagine that you are a *copywriter* hired by an advertising and marketing agency. Your job is to develop the body copy of an ad for your product. Use the steps in the writing process to produce the text that will appear on the ad layout and product package. Be sure to include the following features:

- headline
- slogan
- testimonials
- product description (summary of the product, purposes/uses, important facts, distinguishing features)
- promotional offers and discounts
- contest descriptions and entry forms
- contact information
- procedures/instructions for use

Remember to use vocabulary from the ad word bank and other sources. Be sure to choose words that will reach and persuade your audience. Use compact, effective phrasing that will reduce print costs and build appeal.

Finally, present your ideas in a logical sequence.

© 2003 *Authentic Assessment* by Katherine Luongo-Orlando. Pembroke Publishers. All rights reserved. Permission to reproduce for classroom use.

Creating Body Copy

Headline: _____

Slogan: _____
_____

Testimonials: _____
_____
_____
_____

Product Description: _____
_____

Purposes/Uses _____
_____

Important facts _____
_____

Distinguishing features _____
_____

Summary of the product _____
_____
_____
_____
_____

Promotional Offers and Discounts (optional): _____
_____

Contest Descriptions and Entry Forms (optional): _____
_____
_____

Contact Information (optional): _____
_____

Procedures/Instructions for Use: _____
_____
_____
_____
_____

© 2003 *Authentic Assessment* by Katherine Luongo-Orlando. Pembroke Publishers. All rights reserved. Permission to reproduce for classroom use.

Designing an Ad Layout

Imagine that you are a graphic designer or art director hired by an advertising agency to lay out an ad for your product. Select a template showing the common layout features of a print ad, or develop your own layout design. Arrange important items on the layout. The following items would likely be included:

- headline
- slogan
- logo
- visuals (photo, illustrations)
- product description

- testimonials
- product label
- product character
- contact information

Use a variety of materials and techniques to design your ad layout.

Remember to apply visual elements and symbols to the graphic design features.

Be sure to consider the following items in your design:
- lettering (font)
- size of print
- color

- shapes
- page format
- size of ad

Produce a rough copy of your ad layout. Share it with other art directors and graphic designers—your classmates. Use their feedback to design the final ad layout that will appear in a magazine or newspaper.

© 2003 *Authentic Assessment* by Katherine Luongo-Orlando. Pembroke Publishers. All rights reserved. Permission to reproduce for classroom use.

Ad Layout Templates

HEADLINE

VISUAL

BODY COPY

LOGO AND
SLOGAN

VISUAL

HEADLINE

BODY COPY

LOGO AND
SLOGAN

© 2003 *Authentic Assessment* by Katherine Luongo-Orlando. Pembroke Publishers. All rights reserved. Permission to reproduce for classroom use.

Packaging a Product

Imagine that you are a graphic designer or art director hired by an advertising agency to design a package for your product. Be sure to include important features on the package, such as

- labels, especially the product name
- visuals
- graphics, including a logo
- procedures/instructions
- product description
- quantity of goods and units of measurement
- promotional offers and coupons
- contest descriptions and entry forms
- nutritional information
- other related items

Use a variety of materials and techniques to construct and design the product package. Remember to apply visual elements and symbols to the graphic design features. Be sure to consider the following items in your package design:

- package material
- size and shape of container
- lettering
- size of print
- color
- lines

Produce a rough copy of your package design. Share it with other art directors and graphic designers—your classmates. Use their feedback to construct and design the final package that will appear in supermarkets and other retail stores.

© 2003 *Authentic Assessment* by Katherine Luongo-Orlando. Pembroke Publishers. All rights reserved. Permission to reproduce for classroom use.

5

Gathering Evidence of Student Learning

An important part of the assessment and evaluation process is gathering evidence of students' achievements. Collecting evidence helps teachers and parents discover the strategies and skills that children use to learn and recognize the knowledge they have acquired of key concepts taught. As students take part in learning experiences throughout the year, their performance may vary depending on the instructional activity or assessment task. During the process, children may demonstrate their learning in a variety of ways, and reveal understandings and skills that may not be reflected in a final product or score. Teachers need to be sensitive to such developments. Varying the methods of gathering data will help them appreciate the many facets of students' learning. The range of collection techniques should be utilized over time to adequately represent students' progress. The comprehensive collection of evidence can then be used to produce a balanced and fair assessment of each student.

As children engage in instructional activities and performance tasks, teachers can monitor and collect evidence in ways such as these:

- observing students at work
- making anecdotal notes and comments
- reviewing journal and reflective writing
- having interviews and conversations with students
- collecting work in progress (process work)
- providing for self- and peer-assessments
- assessing final products

Teachers can compile thoughtful collections of evidence using a range of techniques. Acting on some of the following tips will facilitate data gathering:

- Establish a specific time of day for systematic observations of individual students.
- Develop a schedule for observing students (produce a list of students to observe in order and determine a focus for observation), *or*
maintain a clipboard or adhesive notes on hand for continuous record-keeping throughout the day.
- When observing students, note skill development, skill level, and next steps for instruction.

- Interact with students during the learning process by engaging in tasks with them, asking questions, and listening to students at work.
- Hold class meetings, individual or group conferences, or discussions where students can describe their learning to others.
- Ask reflective, thoughtful, and open-ended questions that invite both oral and written response, as in a journal.
- Provide opportunities for students to assess their own work and that of others, using established criteria.
- Encourage students to communicate their learning to parents: they can prepare for and conduct student-led conferences or develop their own progress reports to bring home.
- Collect a variety of final products as concrete evidence of students' learning and date the work samples collected over time.
- Analyze work samples by considering both the content and process involved in developing the final product.

The Creation of Multidimensional Learner Portraits

In order for classroom assessment and evaluation to be reliable and valuable, teachers must collect enough evidence over time to recognize trends and patterns in student learning. Anne Davies, in *Making Classroom Assessment Work*, recommends that teachers gather data using at least three different sources, a process referred to as *triangulation*. In addition to collecting evidence using a range of techniques, educators need to gather information that demonstrates learning and progress over a specific time. In order to develop a multidimensional profile of each child as a learner, parents as well as students should participate in data collection, both at home and at school. All the observations, reflections, conversations, and work done in different learning environments can be used to produce a balanced and holistic assessment of student learning.

Collecting, organizing, and presenting evidence can seem overwhelming to educators, parents, and students alike. However, teachers can develop a variety of tools to help them fulfil the task. They can compile and document information through checklists, inventories, tracking sheets, class lists, adhesive notes, and clipboards. These recording tools can be organized in notebooks, binders, file folders, or portfolios for ongoing access and reference throughout the year.

In order to produce a final assessment and evaluation, teachers need to review the information collected at different stages of the learning process, that is, during the instructional activities and throughout the performance task, and use the evidence they have gathered, along with the assessment results, to determine a final grade or score. In addition to evaluating students' progress, the evidence collected provides educators with reliable information to use for other purposes. Teachers should use the data they have gathered to guide instruction, plan learning experiences, revise teaching strategies, and develop future assessments designed to meet the needs of children in the classroom.

The balance of this chapter provides a range of data collection tools. These have been developed to assist teachers and others with gathering evidence of learning as students engage in the instructional activities and performance tasks featured in this book. Checklists, tracking sheets, conference guidelines, and other recording samples are included for easy use. Teachers can adapt these data gathering tools, or develop their own methods and recording sheets.

Reading Conference General Questions

Throughout the instructional activities, conduct reading conferences with individual students or groups. During a conference, raise questions for discussion that deal with some of the focus topics suggested below. Generate a list of questions specific to a particular book for the reading conference. You might also invite students to read aloud a selected passage from their book to you or the group.

Purpose

Sample Questions:

Why did you choose this book? Was it a good choice? Why or why not?
Would you choose a similar type of book again?

Elements of Story

Sample Questions:

Where does the story take place?
What are some interesting settings in the book?
How does the story begin?
Who is the main character?
Who are some of the other characters?
What happens in the story?
What exciting events take place in the book?
What is the main character's problem or goal?
How is the problem resolved?
How does the story end?

Making Predictions

Sample Questions:

What do you think might happen next? Why do you think this?
What facts or evidence can you provide from the story to support your predictions?

Story Dialogue

Sample Questions:

How does the author use dialogue in the story to explain characters and events?
What interesting conversations take place between the characters?
What important information is revealed in these conversations?

The Author's Use of Words

Sample Question:

What interesting words, phrases, and vocabulary does the author use in the story?

© 2003 *Authentic Assessment* by Katherine Luongo-Orlando. Pembroke Publishers. All rights reserved. Permission to reproduce for classroom use.

Data Gathering Tool

Reading Conference Tracking/Recording Sheets

Names of Students

Criteria/Requirements										
Decides on a purpose for reading										
Selects appropriate reading material										
Reads aloud with fluency and expression										
Identifies basic elements of story										
Explains story conflicts and resolutions										
Retells a story accurately										
Makes predictions using evidence										
Demonstrates reading skills (e.g., sequencing)										
Develops vocabulary by reading										
Uses interesting words and phrases from the book during the reading conference										

Comments:

© 2003 *Authentic Assessment* by Katherine Luongo-Orlando. Pembroke Publishers. All rights reserved. Permission to reproduce for classroom use.

Data Gathering Tool

Reading Class Tracking Sheet

Names of Students

Criteria/Requirements											
Decides on a purpose for reading											
Selects appropriate reading material											
Reads independently											
Responds to literature in a variety of ways											
Reads aloud with fluency and expression											
Identifies basic elements of story											
Explains story conflicts and resolutions											
Makes predictions											
Develops reading strategies/skills (e.g., rereading, sequencing)											
Retells a story accurately											
Expands vocabulary by reading a variety of children's books											
Develops writing skills and style											

© 2003 *Authentic Assessment* by Katherine Luongo-Orlando. Pembroke Publishers. All rights reserved. Permission to reproduce for classroom use.

Map Observation Checklist

Name: _____

Assignment: _____

Date: _____

Observed by

Teacher   Self   Peer   Other

Marked Skills/Behaviors:

✓ Observed   **X** Not observed   **R** Requires assistance

Criteria	Marked Skill/ Behavior		
	✓	**X**	**R**
Title appears neatly on map.			
Content—locations, places, landmarks, and bodies of water—is easy to read and find.			
Information is complete (nothing significant is missing).			
Locations are accurately labelled and placed.			
Legend, symbols, and labels are used appropriately and accurately.			
Areas are colored or shaded neatly.			
Cardinal directions are clearly indicated.			
Scale is used to represent distance or location on map.			

Comments:

© 2003 *Authentic Assessment* by Katherine Luongo-Orlando. Pembroke Publishers. All rights reserved. Permission to reproduce for classroom use.

Writing Observation Checklist

Name: _____ Date: _____

Rating Scale:

4	3	2	1
Always	Usually	Occasionally	Rarely

Criteria	4	3	2	1
Selects own writing topics, ideas, and formats				
Writes for a variety of purposes and audiences				
Incorporates the text features common to the format selected (e.g., procedure, schedule, classified ad)				
Develops content fully and logically, in other words, writes step-by-step instructions and detailed explanations				
Uses sequencing to organize text (e.g., procedural order, chronological list)				
Develops layout, or framework, that is appropriate to the topic and format selected (e.g., procedure, schedule, classified ad)				
Uses appropriate terminology and subject-specific vocabulary				
Uses connecting words to develop coherence and establish sequence				
Maintains tense throughout writing				
Uses parts of speech precisely to explain requirements, procedures, or events				
Applies punctuation and capitalization correctly				
Spells words accurately				
Uses diagrams, illustrations, and other resources to support text and the writing process				
Works with others, including peers, to discuss ideas, revise, and edit work				

Comments:

© 2003 *Authentic Assessment* by Katherine Luongo-Orlando. Pembroke Publishers. All rights reserved. Permission to reproduce for classroom use.

Creating Body Copy Rough Draft Checklist

My rough draft includes the following:	YES	NO
Product Name		
Headline		
Slogan		
Testimonials		
Product Description (summary, uses)		
Target Audience		
An Effective Appeal		
Interesting Words and Phrases		
Additional Information		

© 2003 *Authentic Assessment* by Katherine Luongo-Orlando. Pembroke Publishers. All rights reserved. Permission to reproduce for classroom use.

Creating Body Copy Teacher's Checklist

Student's Name: _____ Grade: _____

Teacher's Name: _____

The student's rough draft includes the following:	YES	NO
Product Name		
Headline		
Slogan		
Testimonials		
Product Description (summary, uses)		
Target Audience		
An Effective Appeal		
Interesting Words and Phrases		
Additional Information		

© 2003 *Authentic Assessment* by Katherine Luongo-Orlando. Pembroke Publishers. All rights reserved. Permission to reproduce for classroom use.

Persuasive Writing and the Media Focus Questions
for Conferences

Throughout the instructional activities, conduct conferences with individual students or small groups. Refer to the sample questions below or generate your own focus questions for discussion.

• What are some examples of persuasive writing found in the media?

• What forms of advertisement do you consider to be most effective in attracting and persuading audiences?

• What is the purpose of ads?

• What techniques are used in advertisements to make them appealing?

• What technique do you consider to be most effective?

• What words do advertisers use to persuade audiences?

• How is *appeal* used to persuade others?

• Name some members of target audiences or consumer groups that products are aimed at.

• How are products developed?

• How is market research conducted? Why?

• Describe some popular products on the market today and explain the effective techniques used to make them appealing.

• What is your favorite advertisement or product? Why?

© 2003 *Authentic Assessment* by Katherine Luongo-Orlando. Pembroke Publishers. All rights reserved. Permission to reproduce for classroom use.

Persuasive Writing and the Media Tracking Sheet

Names of Students

Criteria/Requirements

Criteria/Requirements
Locates examples of persuasive writing in the media (e.g., different forms of advertising)
Understands the purpose of persuasive writing
Identifies characteristics of media products (e.g., text features, design elements)
Identifies techniques used in the media
Selects and uses effective vocabulary to describe media products
Understands basic forms of *appeal*
Identifies target audiences
Recognizes steps in product development
Conducts own market research
Develops own product
Uses various techniques to promote own product
Writes persuasively to convince others
Constructs product packages
Creates graphic designs
Uses effective presentation methods

© 2003 *Authentic Assessment* by Katherine Luongo-Orlando. Pembroke Publishers. All rights reserved. Permission to reproduce for classroom use.

6

Fostering Student Self-Assessment, Reflection, and Goal Setting

Self-assessment, reflection, and goal setting are essential steps in the learning process that build the foundation for students' success. Young people require opportunities to monitor their own understanding, regulate their efforts, measure the quality of their work, and set goals for improvement. Performance-based learning incorporates effective strategies for self-assessment, reflection, and goal setting as part of the evaluation process. As students experience, question, contemplate, and rate their work, they develop higher level thinking skills and learn to strengthen their performance. By critically examining the process and products of their efforts, young people become more aware of the strengths and limitations of their work, accept greater responsibility for the quality of their performance, and gain further control over improving it.

Teachers are responsible for introducing a range of assessment strategies in their classrooms. They can provide effective models, teach the required skills, and allow students to practise them regularly. Initially, self-assessments may involve students in using established criteria to rate their performance. The self-assessment tools on the following pages provide examples of ways that students can rate the quality of their work. With practice, though, learners may develop their own assessment tools, expectations, and standards for excellence to rank their performance independently.

The Development of Independent Thinkers

Through practice in contemplation and guidance, young people can strengthen their ability to reflect on learning experiences, assess achievements, and plan future growth. An important part of the self-assessment, reflection, and goal-setting process is teaching students how metacognition can improve their learning. Through *metacognition*, students are challenged to reflect on the learning process they have engaged in and identify their thinking, learning behaviors, and progress. As part of the process, students think about their thinking, articulate the strategies they use to learn, and become aware of what they know and don't know. Becoming aware of the methods that support their thinking, learning, and development will help students establish goals for success and assist teachers in designing classroom programs that promote learning at its best.

The process of reflection is nurtured through questioning strategies and other metacognitive inquiries. The support systems teachers use to build young people's understanding about their own learning abilities vary depending on the age and individual needs of students. Tools that may be used to promote reflection by students include

- anecdotal response sheets
- checklists
- learning or response logs
- thinking or goal-setting journals
- questionnaires
- inventories
- portfolio entries
- interviews, conferences, small- or large-group discussions
- reflective writing, for example, letters to parents or teachers

Examples of some of these tools for reflection appear in this chapter. They were designed to promote students' self-awareness, consolidate their understandings, acknowledge their personal skills, and extend their learning.

As young people become adept in reflecting on their thinking, monitoring their learning, and understanding their strengths and limitations, they develop lifelong skills in goal setting and metacognition. They become honest, perceptive, and intuitive thinkers who accept responsibility for the quality of work done by looking at it critically over time. As they examine their own work and contrast results with previous samples they have produced, students can witness personal growth through comparison regardless of ability. Making connections, appraising performance, and recognizing areas of weakness are essential steps in establishing personal goals for improvement. Once these personal goals are set, young people should focus on measuring their own achievement towards them, adjusting their efforts, modifying their work, enlisting support when needed, and eventually fulfilling the goals independently. As children move towards independence and build on successful learning experiences, both their performance and self-confidence improve.

While students engage in self-assessment, reflection, and goal setting, teachers can gain insights into how the children learn. The strategies, resources, skills, and understandings that young people identify through a range of metacognitive inquiries can assist educators in planning instruction and developing curriculum that best supports them. In order to establish networks and environments for success, children should be encouraged to share reflection tools, such as letters, questionnaires, and journal entries, with parents, teachers, and peers, in other words, with members of the school community interested in their growth and success. As the education system moves towards authentic practices and performance-based learning, young people should have greater opportunities for thoughtful contemplation, honest assessment, and purposeful goal setting. After all, these classroom experiences carry the potential to shape them into independent, reflective, confident thinkers and achievers capable of adapting to our rapidly changing world.

Reading Survey

1. Listed below are some genres and book topics. Put a check mark next to those that you are most likely to read or are interested in.

Genres

_____ novels

_____ picture books

_____ short stories

_____ myths and legends

_____ fables

_____ folk tales

_____ fairy tales

_____ historical or realistic fiction

_____ science fiction

Other: _____

Topics

_____ animals

_____ relationships

_____ the past

_____ the future

_____ the environment

_____ fantasy

_____ adventure

_____ humor

_____ mystery

Other: _____

2. Make a list of some of your favorite books. _____
_____

3. Who are some of your favorite authors? _____
_____

4. Listed below are some ways of responding to literature. Rank the forms of response you most enjoy in order from 1 to 3. Beside each response format, identify your favorite type of activity.

_____ discussion (e.g., literature circles) _____

_____ writing (e.g., writing-in-role) _____

_____ art (e.g., drama, role play) _____

5. Circle each area in which you believe you need more opportunities to respond to literature.

Discussions about Literature

Interviews

Book talks

Class meetings

Other: _____

Reading conferences/Workshops

Literature circles

Panel discussions

Reading Response Log/Journal

Timelines

Illustrations, diagrams, sketches

Tables, charts, webs

Other: _____

Raising questions

Schedules/Timetables

Maps

© 2003 *Authentic Assessment* by Katherine Luongo-Orlando. Pembroke Publishers. All rights reserved. Permission to reproduce for classroom use.

Writing Activities

Writing-in-role (e.g., diary entries)   Letter writing
Newspaper reports and   Creative spin-offs
    magazine articles   Book reviews
Story sequels and additional chapters   Creative writing (e.g., other works of fiction,
Alternative endings   poetry)

Art Experiences

Visual Arts:
    story illustrations   posters
    watercolor paintings   3-D models
    papier mâché   dioramas
    collages   murals
Other: _____

Music (e.g., creating song medleys)
Dance (e.g., creative movement)
Drama: mime
    tableaux   puppet plays
    improvisation   readers theatre
    role playing   storytelling
    scripts   choral performances

Audio-visual/Media

Animated comic strips   Web sites
Films or screenplays   Video productions
Advertisements   Television programs or commercials
Slide shows   Photo essays

6. Read each statement below. Rank each skill you have developed as

        G Good   **S** Satisfactory   or   **N** Needs improvement.

Circle the letter that represents the quality of your performance.

I can identify basic elements of story.	G	S	N
I can read aloud with fluency.	G	S	N
I can identify story problems and solutions.	G	S	N
I am able to make accurate predictions.	G	S	N
I can retell a story in different ways.	G	S	N
I am developing my vocabulary and writing style from books I have read.	G	S	N

7. What are your overall strengths in reading? _____

    _____

8. What are your goals for improvement? _____

    _____

© 2003 *Authentic Assessment* by Katherine Luongo-Orlando. Pembroke Publishers. All rights reserved. Permission to reproduce for classroom use.

Journal Entry

Type of Journal: **Response**   **Goal Setting**   **Other**
(Circle one.)

Think about the learning activities and performance task you have just finished. Write a journal entry about your experiences. Try to include

- specialized words and subject-specific terms, such as those related to the media or community
- examples
- labelled diagrams
- charts, lists, graphs
- factual information
- detailed descriptions
- complete steps/procedures
- summary of a discussion/conference
- further questions
- other interesting topics

Reflective Letter

Performance Task Completed: _____

Think about the learning activities and performance task you have just completed. Now write a reflective letter, perhaps to your parents or teacher, explaining what you have learned. Refer to this list of topics when writing your letter:

- progress you have made during the assessment unit and performance task
- individual strengths
- areas for growth
- goals for improvement
- personal feelings/emotions about your learning
- methods that help you learn best
- a summary of information you have learned about the topic
- other ways of applying new skills, for example, editorial writing as a type of persuasive writing
- questions you continue to wonder about

Once you have completed your letter, share it with your intended audience. Encourage readers to write a response to the comments and questions within your letter.

© 2003 *Authentic Assessment* by Katherine Luongo-Orlando. Pembroke Publishers. All rights reserved. Permission to reproduce for classroom use.

Persuasive Writing and the Media
Peer Conference Guidelines

Before the Conference

Review the following questions and topics for discussion, and be prepared to share your knowledge and experiences with another student.

- What do you like about your product or ad?
- Describe its functions or uses.
- Identify special features or characteristics.
- What advertising techniques have you used in your layout or package design?
- What techniques or materials might have worked better or more efficiently?
- Explain the problems you encountered and how you overcame them.
- Describe any changes or improvements you made.

During the Conference

Use the vocabulary you acquired while learning about the media and persuasive writing to respond to questions about your ad layout or product. Be sure to explain important concepts, skills, and strategies that you now know.

Following the Conference

Reflect on your discussion and write a response in your notebook or journal. Here are some questions or topics to consider when writing your entry:

- What did you learn by doing this performance task?
- What are your goals for improvement?
- What advice would you give to others about this performance task?
- How might you change the learning activities and final task to make them better for other students? Make a list of your suggestions.
- How can you apply the skills you learned to other tasks/projects?
- What related writing and media topics and projects are you interested in?

© 2003 *Authentic Assessment* by Katherine Luongo-Orlando. Pembroke Publishers. All rights reserved. Permission to reproduce for classroom use.

Reflection Activity

Performance Task Questionnaire

Performance Task Completed: _____

Think about the learning activities and performance task you have just finished.
Now, answer the questions below in the space provided.

What activities did you enjoy most? Why? _____
_____

List three interesting facts you learned about the topic.

1. _____
2. _____
3. _____

What strengths did you demonstrate during the task? _____
_____
_____

What skills have you developed or improved?
How? Describe what you are now able to do that you could not do before.
_____
_____

What activities did you find difficult or challenging? Why? _____
_____
_____

How did you deal with these problems? What strategies did you use?
Describe how other people, materials, and resources helped you with the difficult parts of the task.
_____
_____

How would you change the lessons and performance task? _____
_____
_____

What are your future goals for improvement?

1. _____
2. _____
3. _____

Discuss your responses from the questionnaire with others.
What suggestions from others will help you improve your performance and reach your goals?

1. _____
2. _____
3. _____

© 2003 *Authentic Assessment* by Katherine Luongo-Orlando. Pembroke Publishers. All rights reserved. Permission to reproduce for classroom use.

7

Working Towards a Vision for Assessment

Assessment and evaluation play an important role in guiding instruction and influencing the learning process. The task of gathering information about student performance ought to be shared by teachers and students. As part of the assessment, data should be collected from a variety of sources using effective methods ranging from observations to written samples. Throughout the process, evidence should reflect student growth and program implications.

Symbols or grades usually play an insignificant part in motivating students and promoting learning. However, many school districts and jurisdictions still require teachers to report using letter grades, symbols, or other evaluative feedback. Although learners are closely involved with the assessment of performance, the process of evaluation should remain with teachers. Assigning a score or grade provides educators with a way of combining and reporting information to stakeholders—parents, administrators, and legislators—and developing accountability. The final stages of planning and implementing authentic assessments involve evaluating products, interpreting scores, and sharing results.

To determine the level of performance on the assessment task, use the scoring procedures developed previously. Reconsider the criteria outlined on assessment lists, rating scales, performance checklists, rubrics, and other evaluation tools before examining students' responses. Study the results, keeping these characteristics in mind. Arrange the samples into qualitative groups—good/strong, adequate/satisfactory, weak/insufficient. Examine each group of products and use the analytic or holistic scoring strategy that has been developed or provided to evaluate the responses individually. Consult scoring guidelines or evaluation procedures when available.

Challenges of Reporting Results

The task of implementing rubrics can be challenging for teachers new to performance-based assessment. To evaluate students' responses with rubrics, use the descriptions under each dimension to determine the level of performance. To plot a student accurately on a rubric, all of the performance indicators characteristic of the level of achievement must be demonstrated in the child's response. Although the student's response may indicate some characteristics of other performance levels, plot the student at the lowest level in which all descriptors were accomplished in the task. For example, if a student demonstrates some of the performance criteria for a Level 4 response but all of the performance criteria for a Level 3 response, the student would receive a Level 3 on the assessment task. Similar considerations must be maintained when using developmental rubrics. For instance, if a child indicates some features at the developing stage but all features at the beginning stage, the child is considered to be at the beginning stage.

After evaluating students' achievement on a performance task, teachers using authentic assessment techniques may be faced with a dilemma: transforming their information into a grade for reporting purposes. To do this, you might have to translate the levels of achievement on a rubric into traditional letter grades (a four-level rubric would correspond to letter grades A, B, C, D) or design rubrics to correspond with the number of levels of a particular grading system. For example, qualitative scales that use descriptions such as excellent, good, satisfactory, and needs improvement might correspond to letter grades A, B, C, and D or developmental levels such as exemplary, proficient, progressing, and not meeting the standard.

Rubrics and other evaluative instruments do not always match grading and reporting schemes, however. As a result, teachers may not be able to translate rating scales into percentages, letter grade ranges, or other more familiar systems. In some cases, a numerical score cannot be assigned to performance tasks. Given their complex nature, these tasks are often evaluated in a holistic way. If a grade cannot be assigned, teachers can reveal the contents of the performance task and results in narrative form on the report card. In addition, a copy of the rubric or evaluative instrument may accompany the report card and provide a framework for discussion in an upcoming conference or interview.

The integration of subject matter may present another challenge when reporting grades. Since many assessment tasks involve integrated learning experiences, teachers may be faced with the dilemma of assigning separate grades to different subject areas. To manage this problem successfully, teachers can make one of the following choices:

- use separate rubrics for different aspects of the performance task (e.g., oral presentation, mapping, and writing)
- assign the same grade to subjects that were taught as integrated subjects (e.g., math/science, social studies/personal skills, the arts)
- combine information from rubrics that correspond to the same subject (reading, writing, spelling, and oral presentation could be used for the language arts grade)

In order to produce a grade for report cards, teachers need to factor together a variety of sources of information, such as student products, performances, class participation, unit tests, homework, conferences, self- and peer-assessments, and observations. Samples should be collected early in the reporting period (diagnostic), throughout a unit of study (formative), and late in the reporting period (summative). In order to produce evidence that reflects students' growth and current level of performance, several samples (3–5) need to be gathered over time, dated, and kept in portfolios or other work collections. Once scored, the samples in the portfolio, along with other assessment tools, such as observations and anecdotal comments, should be combined to produce a final grade. Teachers should work within reporting guidelines and assign compulsory letter grades and other evaluative results, when necessary. Always bear in mind, though, to promote learning, students should receive descriptive feedback about their progress.

Effective Communication of Assessment Results

As part of the evaluation and reporting process, teachers must communicate accurate, fair and comprehensive results from authentic assessment practices to students, parents, administrators, and other interested audiences, including politicians. A variety of conference formats can be used to share information effectively. Begin by scheduling a conference with each student at the end of the assessment period. In preparation for the meeting, provide opportunities for learners to review their own work samples and engage in self-assessment and reflection. During the conference, discuss the student's progress by noting individual strengths, improvements in performance, and areas of difficulty. Together, establish plans for future growth.

Throughout the reporting period, provide parents and guardians with copies of the assessment and evaluation tools, along with samples from the performance task, for their review. Shared work samples may include reflections, portfolio collections featuring process work, a photograph or video of students performing, self-assessments, and parent response forms for related feedback.

After the assessment, schedule a parent-teacher conference for sharing results. During the interview, outline the curriculum expectations, examine evidence, including a range of exemplars, and explain how the performance criteria were used to define the student's score. Together, discuss goals for improvement and suggest ways that parents can nurture their child's development at home. These ways include creating a supportive learning environment free from distraction, establishing a routine schedule and time period for completing school work, providing essential resources and materials, practising required skills together that need consolidation, answering questions, reviewing completed work, and offering feedback and encouragement.

One of the most effective ways of communicating assessment results is to hold a parent-teacher-student conference, where a discussion about student achievement is held with all learning partners at once. Since all important members take part in the conference, the participants can review the task requirements, evidence, and scores together before establishing future goals or action plans for improved performance.

As assessment methods and reporting practices continue to change, the format for conducting conferences is also evolving. In recent years, student-led conferencing has become an empowering way for children to take responsibility for their own learning and share their achievements with parents and educators alike. Janet Millar Grant, Barbara Heffler, and Kadri Mereweather, in *Student-Led Conferences*, describe how learners can actively plan, implement, and conduct a reporting conference with the teacher acting as a guide. Teachers can prepare learners to conduct student-led conferences with their parents or guardians by helping them develop portfolios featuring work samples as evidence of their learning; organize an orientation meeting; establish an agenda; schedule conference times; select and display a range of exemplars; teach important skills in effective communication, time management, social behaviors, and conflict resolution; and rehearse for the conference.

The conference format that teachers select for informing parents of assessment results will depend on different factors. To select the communication method you would like to use, consider the current reporting practices in the school, your comfort level and that of your students, the parents' expectations about evaluation and reporting, the frequency of assessments, the duration of reporting periods, and the demands of other interested audiences.

When sharing the results with school administrators, educational decision makers, and other related audiences, it is important to link the criteria on the rubric and performance task requirements to goals and objectives specified in the curriculum. By designing authentic assessments that reflect educational outcomes, teachers can measure student achievement and assess the curriculum to see how it reflects current theories and understandings of how people learn best. In this period of accountability and change, teachers need to work within the regulations for reporting in their schools and districts to satisfy stakeholders in ways that support student achievement and promote best practices.

To use assessment information effectively, teachers should collect evidence, analyze data, and interpret results. By examining the levels of achievement and students' overall performance, teachers can generate work samples that can be used to determine scoring criteria and standards of excellence for future assessments. Assessment evidence can also be used to

- make program modifications, especially for students with special needs
- re-establish goals and evaluation purposes
- improve instructional practices
- locate or reallocate useful resources
- gather support materials to assist learners
- plan lessons, perhaps to consolidate skills and concepts
- revise teaching strategies
- clarify assessment procedures/instructions
- modify performance criteria—combine, eliminate, or add factors
- organize professional development
- facilitate team planning and collaboration, especially for task development and scoring
- develop future assessments, including new performance tasks and evaluation methods

Through reflection, analysis, and collaboration, the assessment information gathered in authentic practices like performance-based learning can be used to guide instruction and develop educational programs that support student learning at its best.

The Value of Authentic Assessment Practices

The move towards authentic assessment practices has lasting implications for students, teachers, and parents. Performance-based learning enables children to demonstrate mastery and competence by engaging in real-life tasks that capture their attention and motivate them to learn. Through self-assessment and reflection, young people can maximize their learning, experience success, develop confidence, and reach independence.

Designing and implementing performance tasks, and the corresponding assessment tools, will help teachers foster their own professional development, improve instructional practices, and build a stronger sense of teamwork with colleagues. Authentic assessment techniques foster dialogue in schools by encouraging team planning and other collaborative initiatives, including team teaching and shared timetabling. These practices enable educators to share ideas, materials, strategies, and resources that support the development and implementation of performance-based learning methods.

Authentic assessment practices increase communication between teachers, students, and parents, too. Task descriptions, performance criteria, evaluation tools, and models of excellence provide frameworks for discussion. Through conferences and other reporting methods, teachers can explain curriculum expectations, scoring strategies, and assessment results with parents and students while establishing learning goals collectively.

School districts and their communities face a great challenge: that of developing a common focus for curriculum, instruction, and assessment. Teachers, parents, students, administrators, and policy makers can meet this by working together to establish a conceptual framework and an educational program that satisfies their goals. A variety of developmental models are available to them.

Performance-based learning and authentic assessment practices embrace a vision of teaching and learning that balances traditional instruction with innovative approaches designed to improve student performance and instructional quality in our schools. As a part of a supportive professional network, let us now work towards this vision.

Performance-Based Assessment Planning

Focus Goal: _____

_____

Learning Objectives/Outcome/Expectations
(content/knowledge, skills, work habits or attitudes)

_____
_____
_____
_____
_____
_____
_____
_____

Task Description

Purpose:

_____
_____

Audience:

_____
_____

Performance Activity:

_____
_____
_____
_____
_____
_____
_____
_____

© 2003 *Authentic Assessment* by Katherine Luongo-Orlando. Pembroke Publishers. All rights reserved. Permission to reproduce for classroom use.

Instructional Activities

_____
_____
_____
_____
_____
_____
_____
_____
_____
_____
_____
_____
_____
_____

Assessment/Evaluation Tool
(scoring procedure)

_____
_____
_____

Directions to Students
(Example: prompts, questions)

_____
_____
_____
_____
_____

Presentation Options/Response Modes

_____
_____
_____
_____
_____

© 2003 _Authentic Assessment_ by Katherine Luongo-Orlando. Pembroke Publishers. All rights reserved. Permission to reproduce for classroom use.

Other Important Considerations (Identify and list.)

Materials and Equipment:

_____

_____

_____

Resources:

_____

_____

_____

_____

_____

_____

Time Allotment: _____

Classroom Organization

Individual Tasks:

_____

_____

_____

Work in Partners/Pairs:

_____

_____

_____

Small-Group Activities:

_____

_____

_____

Large-Group/Whole-Class Activities:

_____

_____

_____

© 2003 *Authentic Assessment* by Katherine Luongo-Orlando. Pembroke Publishers. All rights reserved. Permission to reproduce for classroom use.

Professional Reading

Ainsworth, L., and J. Christinson. 1998. *Student-Generated Rubrics: An Assessment Model to Help All Students Succeed.* Orangeburg, NY: Dale Seymour Publications.

Aker, D. 1995. *Hitting the Mark: Assessment Tools for Teachers.* Markham, ON: Pembroke Publishers.

Anthony, R. J. 1991. *Evaluating Literacy: A Perspective for Change.* Portsmouth, NH: Heinemann Educational.

Booth, D., and G. Olgan. 1996. *Writing Sense: A Teacher's Source Book* (Levels 4 and 6). Toronto: Meadowbook Press.

Bridges, L. 1995. *Assessment: Continuous Learning.* York, ME: Stenhouse Publishers.

Burke, K. 1992. *Authentic Assessment: A Collection.* Palatine, IL: IRI/Skylight Publishing.

Cornfield, R. J., et al. 1987. *Making the Grade: Evaluating Student Progress.* Scarborough, ON: Prentice-Hall.

Davies, A. 2000. *Making Classroom Assessment Work.* Merville, BC: Connections Publishing.

Davies, A., C. Cameron, C. Politano, and K. Gregory. 1992. *Together Is Better: Collaborative Assessment, Evaluation and Reporting.* Winnipeg, MB: Peguis Publishers.

Educators in Connecticut's Pomperaug Regional School District 15. 1996. *A Teacher' Guide to Performance-Based Learning and Assessment.* Alexandria, VA: Association for Supervision and Curriculum Development.

Farr, R., and B. Tone. 1994. *Portfolio and Performance Assessment: Helping Students Evaluate Their Progress as Readers and Writers.* Fort Worth, TX: Harcourt Brace.

Fiderer, A. 1998. *35 Rubrics and Checklists to Assess Reading and Writing: Time Saving Reproducible Forms for Meaningful Literacy Assessment.* New York: Scholastic Professional Books.

Flagg, A. 1998. *Rubrics, Checklists & Other Assessments for the Science You Teach.* New York: Scholastic Professional Books.

Fletcher, R., and J. Portalupi. 1998. *Craft Lessons: Teaching Writing K–8.* York, ME: Stenhouse Publishers.

Glazer, S. M., et al. 1995. *Portfolios and Beyond: Collaborative Assessment in Reading and Writing.* Norwood, MA: Christopher-Gordon Publishers.

Graham, N., and J. George. 1992. *Marking Success: A Guide to Evaluation for Teachers of English*. Markham, ON: Pembroke Publishers.

Grant, J. M., B. Heffler, and K. Mereweather. 1995. *Student-Led Conferences: Using Portfolios to Share Learning with Parents*. Markham, ON: Pembroke Publishers.

Herman, J. L., et al. 1992. *A Practical Guide to Alternative Assessment*. Alexandria, VA: Association for Supervision and Curriculum Development.

Holmes, M. 1993. *The Educator's Guide to Student Evaluation*. Toronto: Ontario Institute for Studies in Education.

Jasmine, J. 1993. *Portfolios and Other Assessments*. Huntington Beach, CA: Teacher Created Materials.

Koechlin, C., and S. Zwaan. 2001. *Info Tasks for Successful Learning: Building Skills in Reading, Writing and Research*. Markham, ON: Pembroke Publishers.

Luongo-Orlando, K. 2001. *A Project Approach to Language Learning: Linking Literary Genres and Themes in Elementary Classrooms*. Markham, ON: Pembroke Publishers.

McLean, J. E., and R. E. Lockwood. 1996. *Why We Access Students—And How: The Competing Measures of Student Performance*. Thousand Oaks, CA: Corwin Press.

McTighe, J., and G. Wiggins. 1999. *Understanding by Design Handbook*. Alexandria, VA: Association for Supervision and Curriculum Development.

Ogle, D. "K-W-L: A Teaching Model That Develops Active Reading of Expository Texts." *The Reading Teacher* 39: 564–70.

Olgan, G., et al., eds. 1996. *Writing Sense: Your Writing Skills Handbook* (Student Editions, Books 4 and 6). Toronto: Meadowbook Press.

Portalupi, J., and R. Fletcher. 2001. *Nonfiction Craft Lessons: Teaching Information Writing K–8*. Portland, ME: Stenhouse Publishers.

Raison, G., et al. 1994. *First Steps Writing: Resource Book*. Australia: Longman House.

Tarrart, G. L., et al. 1998. *Rubrics: A Handbook for Construction and Use*. Lancaster, PA: Technomic Publishing.

Toronto District School Board. 2000. *Integrated Assessment Instruction and Reporting*. Toronto: Toronto District School Board.

Wiggins, G. 1992. "Creating Tests Worth Taking." *Readings from Educational Leadership: Performance Assessment*. Ed. by Ronald S. Brandt. Alexandria, VA: Association for Supervision and Curriculum Development.

Wiggins, G., and J. McTighe. 1998. *Understanding by Design*. Alexandria, VA: Association for Supervision and Curriculum Development.

Acknowledgments

Early in my professional career, I was part of the development team for a systematic authentic assessment program for my former school board. During that time, I had the opportunity to work with talented educators and experienced research staff on the design of performance tasks, rubrics, and administration and scoring procedures for assessments in language arts. My thanks go to Vince DePasquale and the other professionals I had the pleasure of working with on this project. The experiences we shared have become the cornerstone of this book.

Authentic Assessment: Designing Performance-Based Tasks would never have come to be without the profound influence and support of many educators, professionals, colleagues, and friends. Thank you to the staff of the TDSB Professional Library, for assisting with the months of research that helped build the knowledge base needed to write this book. Special thanks to John Glossop, for continuing to share resources and experiences that support my work with children and teachers.

Throughout my teaching career, I have had the privilege of working with many dedicated teachers, whose classrooms are an inspiring source of creativity and learning. Special thanks to Danielle Honour for facilitating my work on this book. The learning experiences with which you provided your students helped me recognize children's outstanding potential. Your initiative, support, and thoughtful reflections will always have an influence on my life and work.

The enriching classroom experiences I have had over the years have led to my work as a writer. Thank you to the students of John D. Parker Public School and Smithfield Middle School, whose enthusiasm, interest, and work set the foundation for this book. The samples you have created will serve as models of excellence for years to come.

Thank you to the staff at Pembroke Publishers, especially Mary Macchiusi, whose insight and faith convinced me I had another book in the making. Your vision, guidance, and patience helped shape the pages and chapters others would read.

Special thanks to my editor, Kate Revington, whose editorial leadership, professionalism, and attention to detail have provided me with some of the most skilled lessons on writing.

Throughout my life, I have been blessed with many gifts. My greatest blessings have been my family and friends, who have shared my life and work. Publishing this book would not have been possible without any of them.

Thank you to my wonderful mentors, Gillda Leitenberg, Joan Fulford, and Emma DeTommaso, who continue to support me in all aspects of my life. Your guidance and friendship have been a source of enrichment and inspiration.

Thank you to the circle of friends and family members whose constant help and encouragement guided me through the many stages of my writing. Your interest and support gave me the motivation to continue. Special thanks to my mother, whose memory and love remain as strong as her legacy.

Thank you to my husband Matteo, for your unwavering strength and guidance. Your support, understanding, and patience made it possible for me to write another book at a time when so much was changing. Thanks for being my greatest help and biggest fan.

Finally, thank you to my daughter, Issabella Victoria, whose love for language, enjoyment of literature, and interest in learning have inspired me to continue my life's work as a mother, author, and teacher.

Index

942012